AFRICAN POLITICAL, ECONOMIC, AND SECURITY ISSUES

TUNISIA

TRANSITION AND CHALLENGES

AFRICAN POLITICAL, ECONOMIC, AND SECURITY ISSUES

Additional books in this series can be found on Nova's website under the Series tab.

Additional E-books in this series can be found on Nova's website under the E-book tab.

GLOBAL POLITICAL STUDIES

Additional books in this series can be found on Nova's website under the Series tab.

Additional E-books in this series can be found on Nova's website under the E-book tab.

AFRICAN POLITICAL, ECONOMIC, AND SECURITY ISSUES

TUNISIA

TRANSITION AND CHALLENGES

HOWARD SANCHEZ
AND
RUSSELL FREEMAN
EDITORS

New York

For permission to use material from this book please contact us:
Telephone 631-231-7269; Fax 631-231-8175
Web Site: http://www.novapublishers.com

Library of Congress Cataloging-in-Publication Data

ISBN: 978-1-62417-755-2

Published by Nova Science Publishers, Inc. † New York

CONTENTS

Preface		**vii**
Chapter 1	Political Transition in Tunisia *Alexis Arieff*	**1**
Chapter 2	The Prospects for Security Sector Reform in Tunisia: A Year after the Revolution *Querine Hanlon*	**31**
Index		**69**

PREFACE

The departure of longtime President Zine el Abidine Ben Ali in January 2011, in the face of massive anti-government protests, was greeted with euphoria within Tunisia and sparked opposition and reform movements across the region. Yet despite significant accomplishments since that time, Tunisians today face a wide range of challenges, including economic hardship, relatively impoverished interior, and the security implications of events in neighboring Libya. Domestic tensions between Islamists and secularists have also burgeoned. This book explores Tunisia's transition and the future of the country and the region, with a focus on: the struggle between reformists and entrenched forces carried over from the former regime; the potential shape of the new political system; the role and influence of Islamism in the government and society; the question of how to transform the formerly repressive security services; and the difficult diplomatic balance, for the U.S. and other actors, of encouraging greater democratic openness while not undermining other foreign policy priorities.

Chapter 1 – The departure of longtime President Zine el Abidine Ben Ali in January 2011, in the face of massive anti-government protests, was greeted with euphoria within Tunisia and sparked opposition and reform movements across the region. Yet despite significant accomplishments since that time, Tunisians today face a wide range of challenges, including economic hardship, disputes over reform priorities, labor unrest, tensions between the privileged coastal region and relatively impoverished interior, and the security implications of events in neighboring Libya. Domestic tensions between Islamists and secularists have also burgeoned. Elections held in October 2011 to select a National Constituent Assembly provided momentum to a transition process that has at times appeared slow and unwieldy. The Assembly is expected to draft a new constitution ahead of new elections currently slated for early 2013. Al Nahda (alt: Ennahda/AnNahda), a moderate Islamist party, won 41% of the seats in the October vote, and is ruling in a coalition with two secular parties. The coalition is subject to internal frictions due to the three parties' divergent histories and policy preferences.

Tunisia's transition raises a wide range of questions for the future of the country and the region. These pertain to the struggle between reformists and entrenched forces carried over from the former regime; the potential shape of the new political system; the role and influence of Islamism in the government and society; the question of how to transform the formerly repressive security services; and the difficult diplomatic balance—for the United States and other actors—of encouraging greater democratic openness while not undermining other foreign policy priorities. Tunisia exhibits a number of unique attributes within the region: a relatively small territory, a sizable and well educated middle class, and a long history of encouraging women's socioeconomic freedoms. Some policymakers view these factors as advantageous, and describe Tunisia as a potential "test case" for democratic transitions in the region. Tunisia's example may nonetheless be less influential than larger or more central states such as Egypt and Syria.

Congress authorizes and appropriates foreign assistance funding and oversees U.S. foreign policy toward Tunisia and the wider region. The Obama Administration has indicated a desire to deepen ties with Tunisia, including by encouraging increased trade and investment, and U.S. bilateral aid has significantly expanded to assist the country with its transition. As part of this transition support, the State Department is providing Tunisia with a $100 million cash transfer to help cover its debt payments. Prior to 2011, U.S.-Tunisian relations were highly focused on military assistance and counterterrorism. International financial institutions, which receive significant U.S. funding, have also pledged aid for Tunisia. Some Members of Congress argue that additional aid should be allocated for democracy promotion and economic recovery in Tunisia, while others contend that budgetary cuts take precedence over new aid programs, or that economic stabilization may be best addressed by the private sector or by other donors. P.L. 112-74, the FY2012 Consolidated Appropriations Act, contains provisions relevant to Tunisia. Relevant pending legislation includes H.Res. 527 (Murphy); S.Res. 316 (Lieberman); S. 1388 (Kerry); and S. 3241 and H.R. 5857, draft versions of the FY2013 Department of State, Foreign Operations, and Related Programs Appropriations Act.

Chapter 2 – In the year since the revolution, Tunisia has achieved what no other Arab Spring country has managed: peaceful transition to democratic rule through national elections widely viewed to be free and fair. The legacy of the previous regime, however, remains: a complete lack of transparency, no real parliamentary or government oversight, and largely unchanged rules of engagement and training. Tunisia's internal security services are feared by the population and are themselves fearful of fulfilling their basic policing tasks. The Tunisian Armed Forces clearly ascribe to the concept of civilian oversight of the military. Although they are currently fulfilling a number of internal security tasks, they have publicly stated their intention to return to the barracks when the police can resume responsibility for internal security. Security sector reform (SSR) will be critical for building trust in the new government and its security institutions. The *raison d'être* of Ben Ali's security institutions was to protect the regime, not the population. SSR is essential for reorienting the mandate and institutional culture of Tunisia's labyrinth of security institutions. Serious reform of the security sector is essential if Tunisia's transition to democratic rule is to succeed in the long term.

In: Tunisia: Transition and Challenges
Editors: H. Sanchez and R. Freeman
ISBN: 978-1-62417-755-2

Chapter 1

POLITICAL TRANSITION IN TUNISIA*

Alexis Arieff

SUMMARY

The departure of longtime President Zine el Abidine Ben Ali in January 2011, in the face of massive anti-government protests, was greeted with euphoria within Tunisia and sparked opposition and reform movements across the region. Yet despite significant accomplishments since that time, Tunisians today face a wide range of challenges, including economic hardship, disputes over reform priorities, labor unrest, tensions between the privileged coastal region and relatively impoverished interior, and the security implications of events in neighboring Libya. Domestic tensions between Islamists and secularists have also burgeoned. Elections held in October 2011 to select a National Constituent Assembly provided momentum to a transition process that has at times appeared slow and unwieldy. The Assembly is expected to draft a new constitution ahead of new elections currently slated for early 2013. Al Nahda (alt: Ennahda/AnNahda), a moderate Islamist party, won 41% of the seats in the October vote, and is ruling in a coalition with two secular parties. The coalition is subject to internal frictions due to the three parties' divergent histories and policy preferences.

Tunisia's transition raises a wide range of questions for the future of the country and the region. These pertain to the struggle between reformists and entrenched forces carried over from the former regime; the

* This is an edited, reformatted and augmented version of Congressional Research Service, Publication No. RS21666, dated June 18, 2012.

potential shape of the new political system; the role and influence of Islamism in the government and society; the question of how to transform the formerly repressive security services; and the difficult diplomatic balance—for the United States and other actors—of encouraging greater democratic openness while not undermining other foreign policy priorities. Tunisia exhibits a number of unique attributes within the region: a relatively small territory, a sizable and well educated middle class, and a long history of encouraging women's socioeconomic freedoms. Some policymakers view these factors as advantageous, and describe Tunisia as a potential "test case" for democratic transitions in the region. Tunisia's example may nonetheless be less influential than larger or more central states such as Egypt and Syria.

Congress authorizes and appropriates foreign assistance funding and oversees U.S. foreign policy toward Tunisia and the wider region. The Obama Administration has indicated a desire to deepen ties with Tunisia, including by encouraging increased trade and investment, and U.S. bilateral aid has significantly expanded to assist the country with its transition. As part of this transition support, the State Department is providing Tunisia with a $100 million cash transfer to help cover its debt payments. Prior to 2011, U.S.-Tunisian relations were highly focused on military assistance and counterterrorism. International financial institutions, which receive significant U.S. funding, have also pledged aid for Tunisia. Some Members of Congress argue that additional aid should be allocated for democracy promotion and economic recovery in Tunisia, while others contend that budgetary cuts take precedence over new aid programs, or that economic stabilization may be best addressed by the private sector or by other donors.

P.L. 112-74, the FY2012 Consolidated Appropriations Act, contains provisions relevant to Tunisia. Relevant pending legislation includes H.Res. 527 (Murphy); S.Res. 316 (Lieberman); S. 1388 (Kerry); and S. 3241 and H.R. 5857, draft versions of the FY2013 Department of State, Foreign Operations, and Related Programs Appropriations Act.

OVERVIEW

In the second year of their country's transition from authoritarian rule, Tunisians can point to a number of significant achievements—not least, the holding of widely praised national elections in October 2011 that put in place a National Constituent Assembly.[1] Since the end of the regime of former President Zine el Abidine Ben Ali, political prisoners have been released, over 100 new political parties have been authorized, and most online and media restrictions have been lifted.

Source: Map Resources, adapted by CRS.

Figure 1. Map of Tunisia.

The former ruling party has been dissolved and its funds liquidated, and a number of former officials and Ben Ali associates and relatives have been arrested or charged in absentia.

Still, Tunisians face a wide range of challenges, including economic hardship, disputes over policy priorities, labor unrest, tensions between the privileged coastal region and relatively impoverished interior, and the security implications of events in neighboring Libya. Tunisian elites appear to agree on the need to dismantle and reform authoritarian structures while resisting a political witch-hunt. Yet progress in some areas—notably reform of the internal security services and judiciary—has been slow.[2] Tunisia's leaders are also trying to respond to pressing socioeconomic problems—such as acute regional inequality; high unemployment; and the collapse of the tourism industry, a key economic driver—while reassuring international partners that they will not pursue overly populist or religiously conservative policies that could harm foreign investors. Tunisians continue to grapple with how best to approach issues such as transitional justice, regional and internal security threats, and the creation of new electoral institutions.[3]

The moderate Islamist party Al Nahda (alt: Ennahda/An-Nahda, "Renaissance") won 89 seats in the Constituent Assembly—by far the largest block—and is leading a ruling coalition with the center-left, secular Congress for the Republic (CPR) and Ettakatol (Democratic Forum of Labor and Liberties or FDTL). Ettakatol leader Mustapha Ben Jaafar is serving as president of the Assembly, CPR leader Moncef Marzouki as president, and Al Nahda's secretary-general, Hamadi Jebali, as prime minister—the head of government and most powerful of the three roles. This "Troika" coalition is subject to internal frictions, given the leading figures' divergent histories and policy preferences. The left-leaning, stringently secularist Progressive Democratic Party (PDP) is spear-heading the opposition to Al Nahda within the Assembly.

The 217-seat Constituent Assembly is charged with drafting a new constitution, performing quasi-legislative functions, and preparing for future parliamentary and/or presidential elections, which will formally signal the next step in the transition process. The government has indicated that these elections will be held in early 2013, pending the completion of the constitution drafting and adoption process. Areas of focus for the constitution include the future system of government (parliamentary, presidential, or a combination), the shape of internal checks-and-balances, the role and structure of the judiciary, the level of protection for individual rights, and the relationship between religion and state. While parliamentarians have solicited some civil society input on the constitution, the prospects for broad-based public consultation appear slim.[4]

Complex tensions among Islamists and secularists have escalated in recent months. Trade unions, media advocates, and some civil society groups accuse Al Nahda of seeking to exert political control over state institutions, restrict unflattering news coverage, and intimidate critics. Al Nahda supporters, meanwhile, view some critics as immovably opposed to Islamist groups and argue that stringently secular elites have lost their claim on popular legitimacy.

Al Nahda leaders have simultaneously struggled to respond to conservative critics who accuse them of abdicating their responsibility to institute a greater public role for Islam. At the root of these debates are questions of how Tunisia's new democracy will interpret certain democratic principles such as freedom of speech and define the role of religion in political life. Recent violence by Salafists has increased pressure on the government to ensure public order and weigh in on controversial social issues.

Resurgent public demonstrations, strikes, and riots over economic conditions are ongoing challenges, particularly in the interior. Tunisia's main trade union federation, the UGTT, has attempted to assert its influence by positioning itself as a channel for widespread economic grievances and a counter-weight to Al Nahda. At times, police have cracked down violently on political protests, including on several occasions this year. Government officials, for their part, have unsuccessfully called for a social "truce," blaming protests for obstructing economic recovery. At times, the government's internal divisions and the ambiguity of its mandate have impeded its ability to react quickly and decisively to events. Dissatisfaction and confusion over the transition process could resurface as elites continue to confront debates over who is empowered to act and how to deliver tangible benefits to an impatient public with vast and divided expectations. A recent analysis by the International Crisis Group warned that socioeconomic insecurity and political instability could "negatively feed on each other and risk snowballing into a legitimacy crisis" for the elected government.[5]

BACKGROUND

Tunisia's "Jasmine Revolution" began with mounting anti-government protests in the country's interior in December 2010 and culminated in the decision of President Ben Ali, in power since 1987, to flee the country for Saudi Arabia on January 14, 2011 (see text-box below). Tunisia's popular uprising inspired reform and opposition movements throughout the region. These democracy movements have been internationally heralded, but they have also complicated longstanding policies and assumptions.[6]

The early months of Tunisia's transition were marked by ongoing unrest, partly in response to the initial dominance of officials from the former regime in the interim government. A security vacuum additionally raised fears of violence and chaos. In February 2011, a more stable, if weak, interim government took shape under Prime Minister Béji Caïd Essebsi, an elder statesman from the administration of founding President Habib Bourguiba. Caïd Essebsi introduced the idea, popular with protesters, of electing an assembly to write a new constitution— that is, forge a new political system— before holding parliamentary and/or presidential polls.

Tunisia at a Glance

Population: 10.7 million (July 2011 est.)
Income Level: Lower middle income
Urbanization rate: 67% of the population (2010)
Life Expectancy: 75 years (2011 est.)
Religion: Muslim: 98%, Christian: 1%, Jewish and other, 1%
Literacy: 78% (2008)
Key Exports: clothing, semi-finished goods (notably spare automotive parts), textiles, agricultural products
Key Imports: textiles, machinery and equipment, hydrocarbons
Major Trading Partners: France, Italy, Germany, Libya, China, Spain
Female Labor Participation Rate (% of female population): 25% (2009)

Sources: CIA, The World Factbook; World Bank, World Development Indicators.

Prior to January 2011, Tunisia was widely viewed as exhibiting a stable, albeit authoritarian, regime that focused on economic growth while staving off political liberalization. It had had only two leaders since gaining independence from France in 1956: the late Habib Bourguiba, a secular nationalist who helped lead Tunisia's independence movement, and Ben Ali, a former interior minister and prime minister who assumed the presidency in 1987. Ben Ali cultivated the internal security services and the Constitutional Democratic Rally (RCD) party as his power base, and placed severe restrictions on human rights, political participation, and freedom of expression. The president and his family were also seen as highly corrupt.

While Tunisia shares many characteristics with neighboring countries, some are unique: a small territory, a relatively homogenous population (despite tribal and ethnic divisions in some areas), a liberalized economy, a large and educated middle class, and a history of encouraging women's socioeconomic freedoms.[7] Arabic-speaking Sunni Muslims make up the overwhelming majority of Tunisia's population, but its urban culture and elite reflect a strong European influence. The population is young compared with developed countries, but its youth bulge is declining.[8] As many as 1 million Tunisians reside abroad, mainly in Europe.

The legal and socioeconomic status of women in Tunisia are among its particularities. Polygamy is banned, and women enjoy equal citizenship rights and the right to initiate divorce. (That said, inheritance laws and practices are generally disadvantageous to women.) Women serve in the military and in many professions, and constitute more than 50% of university students; the first woman governor was appointed in 2004. Many credit the country's relatively liberal Personal Status Code, promulgated under founding President Bourguiba, with these advances.

Despite its apparent relative prosperity, Tunisia has long exhibited a significant divide between rural and urban areas, and especially between the developed, tourist-friendly coast and the poorer interior. At least half of the population lives in Tunis and coastal towns, and there is population drift toward these areas. Anti-government unrest, particularly rooted in labor and economic grievances, has often originated in the interior—as did the protests that unseated Ben Ali.

The "Jasmine Revolution"

Protests were first reported on December 17, 2010, in the interior town of Sidi Bouzid, after a 26-year-old street vendor named Mohamed Bouazizi set himself on fire to protest police interference and a lack of economic opportunities. Feeding on local anger over high unemployment and a lack political and socioeconomic freedoms, and leveraged by underground networks of activists, hackers, and dissidents, the demonstrations escalated into an unprecedented popular challenge to the Ben Ali regime. Public demonstrations had previously been very rare in Tunisia, due to state repression and pervasive surveillance. From the start, protesters appeared to lack a central leader and were not aligned with a pre-existing political or ideological movement.

Protests erupted in Tunis in early January, and rioters ransacked private properties belonging to Ben Ali's wealthy relatives along the central coast, underscoring the deep antipathy many Tunisians felt toward members of the ruling elite. Authorities imposed a state of emergency, and police repeatedly opened fire on crowds and arrested protesters, journalists, opposition party members, lawyers, and rights advocates, some of whom were reportedly abused in detention. According to recently released figures, 338 people were killed in the uprising.[9]

Prior to his exile, Ben Ali offered a series of concessions on political and civil rights in an effort to stem the unrest. On January 13, the president gave an address on national television in which he pledged to step down when his term was up in 2014, to allow fresh parliamentary elections before then, and to end state censorship. However, these promises did not placate demonstrators. On January 14, 2011, Ben Ali fled in a private plane for Saudi Arabia.

Key Issues

Islam, Politics, and the State

Tunisian Islamists and secularists have grown increasingly polarized since the 2011 uprising. The October 2011 election results confirmed the rise of Al Nahda, a moderate Islamist movement founded in the 1980s by Rachid Ghannouchi and Abdelfattah Mourou.[10] Al Nahda won 37% of the popular vote, more than the next eight parties combined.[11] The party has therefore found itself at the center of emerging debates over religion, state, and identity. Al Nahda leaders portray themselves as moderates who espouse democratic participation, support the separation of religion and state, oppose religious extremism, and seek to preserve and expand women's freedoms. Yet the party appears to be facing internal divisions while also potentially competing with emergent, more radical Islamist groups for popular support. Ghannouchi has said that he will soon step down as Al Nahda's president, placing its future direction in question. Secularist detractors accuse the party of "double discourse," that is, of displaying moderation in order to enter government and reassure foreign partners, but intending to gradually introduce restrictive laws and institutions. Critics have also accused Al Nahda of seeking to dominate the political system and allege that Arab Gulf states—notably Qatar—are using the party as a tool to influence events in Tunisia.[12] Conversely, Al Nahda members purport to feel threatened by leftist and secular elite actors, whom they accuse of seeking illegitimately to restrict Islamists' political influence.

Debate over the role of *sharia* (Islamic law) illustrates the challenges inherent in navigating Islamist/secularist divisions within the Constituent Assembly. In February, Al Nahda parliamentarians proposed enshrining *sharia* as the source of Tunisian law, contrary to indications from party leaders during the electoral campaign that they would instead retain Article 1 of Tunisia's old constitution (which states that Tunisia's "religion is Islam, its language is Arabic, and its type of government is the Republic") as an unenforceable statement of Tunisian identity. Conservative Islamists held large demonstrations in support of the proposal, while Assembly Speaker Ben Jaafar threatened to resign if the proposal were adopted. In March, Al Nahda leaders announced they would not support the reference to *sharia*, and reaffirmed their support for the original Article 1 wording. This decision was cheered by secularist parties and was seen by some as a victory for moderate voices within the party.[13] Some conservatives, however, viewed the outcome as a betrayal. Similar debates may emerge over the mandate of the Ministry of Religious Affairs, which regulates religious activities; the legal status of religiously conservative Salafist groups; the status of religious minorities (there are tiny Jewish and Christian communities); and how to balance freedom of expression and religious sensitivities.

Religiously conservative Salafists have become more visible in the post-Ben Ali era, and have challenged the government and liberals through protests, threats, and at times violence.[14] Ghannouchi and other Al Nahda figures in early 2012 stated that the party was engaging Salafists in a dialogue aimed at eventually bringing them into the political system, while emphasizing that violence and jihadist ideology would not be tolerated.[15] Al Nahda's critics have accused it of not doing enough to prevent and punish Salafists who seek to intimidate secular activists, university professors, and political opponents. Such criticisms underscore the party's difficult path between mollifying moderate and secularist Tunisians—and international partners—while potentially seeking to retain legitimacy among more radical segments of the population.

In recent months, Salafist agitation and violence have increased, while the government has taken a harder line. In May 2012, thousands attended a "national conference" organized by the Salafist group Ansar al Sharia in the Islamic holy city of Kairouan. Ansar al Sharia (which shares a name with extremist groups based elsewhere) was founded by a former member of the Tunisian Combatant Group, a recently dormant entity that was formerly a U.S.-designated foreign terrorist organization (see "Security Concerns," below). The same month, Salafists attacked alcohol vendors in the central town of Sidi Bouzid, and in mid-June, Salafist groups in and around Tunis rioted, sacked leftist political party and union offices, and violently clashed with police following an art exhibit they deemed offensive to Islam.[16] In May, Prime Minister Jebali and Interior Minister Ali Laraydh warned that the government would not hesitate to use force to instill order. Following the June riots, the government threatened to use Tunisia's anti-terror law (criticized for its expansive use under Ben Ali) against those who employ violence. At the same time, government officials condemned the art exhibit's "attacks on religion," and have suggested they might include language barring offense to religion in the draft constitution.[17]

Background on Al Nahda

Led by Islamic scholar and activist Rachid Ghannouchi, Al Nahda was founded in 1981—soon after multiparty politics were legalized under President Bourguiba—as the Islamic Tendency Movement (MTI). The MTI organized demonstrations on university campuses and engaged in clashes with security forces and with leftist groups. The growing unrest, coming on the heels of mass protests and strikes by trade unions, undermined support for Bourguiba and laid the groundwork for Ben Ali's rise in 1987.[18] Upon coming to power, Ben Ali promised greater pluralism and a dialogue with opposition groups. Al Nahda candidates were permitted to run as independents in the 1989 parliamentary elections, but Ben Ali initiated a crackdown when they garnered 15% of the national vote. Clashes between the government and Al Nahda activists escalated, culminating in an attack on a ruling party office in 1991 that the government blamed on Al Nahda.

The government subsequently claimed it had unearthed an Islamist plot to assassinate Ben Ali, and in 1992 Tunisian military courts convicted hundreds of Al Nahda members. Al Nahda leaders denied the accusations, and some rights advocates criticized the case as biased and lacking due process.[19] Ghannouchi, who had left the country, was sentenced in absentia. Similar tensions between Islamists and government forces drove neighboring Algeria into civil war in the early 1990s.

Al Nahda's electoral success in 2011 appears to have stemmed from several factors. Clearly, the movement remained popular despite decades of confinement to exile and underground activities, and its message of reconciling Islam and democracy appears to enjoy broad appeal in Tunisia. In addition, the repression meted out to the group under Ben Ali appears to have endeared the movement to many Tunisians and enhanced its popular legitimacy.

Al Nahda did not play a significant role in the "Jasmine Revolution" uprising, but the organization raised its profile in 2011 through a series of politically savvy choices.

Al Nahda is widely reported to have engaged in superior grassroots mobilization during the electoral campaign, and may have benefitted from campaign missteps by the most vocally secularist parties. These parties attempted to drive a wedge between Islamists and secularists, a strategy that may have backfired among Tunisians eager to reconcile democracy with their Arab/Muslim identity.

Calls for Justice, Reform, and Accountability

Tunisian authorities continue to grapple with how best to ensure accountability for past abuses while encouraging national reconciliation. Some 2 million Tunisians were reportedly members of the former ruling party; selecting who should face sanction is therefore a challenge. Numerous criminal charges have been brought against Ben Ali and his wife, Leila Trabelsi, both of whom remain outside the country, along with dozens of family members and former government and security officials.

An ad-hoc commission appointed during the interim government carried out an investigation into corruption under the former regime; its final report, submitted in November 2011, may lead to new prosecutions. Yet, many Tunisians are skeptical regarding the justice system, which was inherited from the Ben Ali regime and is widely viewed as politicized, ineffective, and in some cases corrupt.[20]

Meanwhile, the families of victims in the 2011 uprising have become increasingly vocal in demanding state compensation and justice.

A central policy challenge facing Tunisia's new leaders is the question of how to assert control over the size and mandate of the internal security services, without sowing future instability.

It may also take time before members of the public are willing to trust the police to ensure their security. The Interior Ministry oversees the security and intelligence services, along with the police; all were closely associated with Ben Ali and with abuses such as extrajudicial arrests, extensive internet surveillance, and torture.

Progress on security sector reform has been slow, and to date, little information has been made public regarding the security apparatus's internal structure or staffing. Moreover, signs of tension within the Interior Ministry, now headed by an Al Nahda official but largely staffed by holdovers from the former regime, have emerged.[21]

Security Concerns

Although the security situation has largely stabilized in Tunis and other major urban centers, protests, riots, and other disturbances have surged in recent months, particularly in the dispossessed areas of the interior where the 2011 uprising started. Such episodes appear to indicate widespread dissatisfaction with the lack of tangible socioeconomic benefits since the revolution. Insecurity along the borders with Libya and Algeria is of additional concern amid reports of increased regional weapons trafficking linked to the collapse of the Qadhafi regime, and of increasingly armed smuggling operations in general.[22] To some extent, policing Tunisia's sparse southern desert regions may present a security challenge for years to come.

Recent months have seen public appearances by Tunisian nationals implicated in terrorist activities abroad, including Tarek Maaroufi of the Tunisian Combatant Group (TCG, see below), who returned to Tunisia in April 2012 after being released from prison in Belgium. News reports have since linked Maaroufi to the participation of Tunisians in armed opposition activities in Syria, although his current whereabouts are unclear.[23] Another former TCG figure, Seif Allah ben Hassine (alt: Sayf Allah Bin Hussayn, aka Abu Iyadh), is a leader in the Tunisian Salafist group Ansar al Sharia (see "Islam, Politics, and the State" above). These individuals' intentions are uncertain. As mentioned above, Al Nahda officials have recently taken a harder tone toward Tunisian Salafists who have used violence, but the handling of such groups remains a policy challenge.

Some analysts fear that Al Qaeda in the Islamic Maghreb (AQIM), a regional criminal/terrorist group with roots in Algeria's 1990s civil conflict, could take advantage of political instability, upheaval in Libya, and disorder among Tunisia's security services. AQIM released a statement in January 2011 hailing the departure of Ben Ali and warning against supposed U.S. and French efforts to subvert the revolution.[24] Tunisian forces have clashed with militants described as affiliated with AQIM several times in the past year.[25] Al Qaeda's second-in-command, Ayman al Zawahiri, has released at least two statements seeking to portray uprisings in Tunisia and Egypt as motivated by Islamist sentiment and warning that the United States would seek to manipulate the outcomes; in June 2012, Zawahiri called on Tunisians to rise up against Al Nahda for accepting a constitution not based on *sharia*.[26] Al Nahda leader Ghannouchi responded that Zawahiri "has no influence in Tunisia," adding, "this man is a disaster for Islam and for Muslims."[27]

Tunisia's military, totaling roughly 35,000 personnel, has historically received fewer state resources than the internal security services, and Tunisians view it as relatively apolitical. Senior army officers—notably, General Rachid Ammar, then army chief of staff (since promoted to military chief of staff)—reportedly refused orders to open fire on demonstrators during the January 2011 uprising, thereby influencing Ben Ali's decision to step down.[28] On January 23, Ammar publicly addressed protesters and promised to safeguard Tunisia's "revolution." While Ammar's comments were welcomed by many Tunisians, they sparked concern among some observers over whether the armed forces might interfere in domestic politics, particularly if the security situation should worsen.[29] The military has since led internal and border security efforts amid attempts to establish police capacity and professionalism. The army remains popular, but this enlarged role could cause the relatively small armed forces to become overstretched.

Terrorism in Tunisia: Background

While Tunisia has not been subject to many large attacks, terrorism is a potential domestic threat and some Tunisian nationals have participated in plots abroad. Two notable incidents on Tunisian soil were the 2002 bombing of a synagogue on the Tunisian island of Djerba (noted for its tiny Jewish population) and a series of street battles between alleged militants and security forces in Tunis in December 2006-January 2007. Al Qaeda deputy leader Ayman al Zawahiri appeared to claim responsibility for the Djerba bombing in a taped message broadcast in October 2002. In all, 14 German tourists, 5 Tunisians, and 2 French citizens were killed in the attack.[30] France, Spain, Italy, and Germany arrested expatriate Tunisians for alleged involvement. The roots of the 2006- 2007 violence, in which 14 militants were reported killed, are more opaque.

In 2002, the U.S. State Department placed the Tunisian Combatant Group (TCG), which operated outside Tunisia, on a list of specially designated global terrorists and froze its assets.[31] The TCG sought to establish an Islamic state in Tunisia and was suspected of plotting attacks on the U.S., Algerian, and Tunisian embassies in Rome in December 2001. One founder, Tarek Maaroufi, was arrested in Belgium the same month. The group appears to have since been inactive. Maaroufi, however, has since been released and recently returned to Tunisia (see above).

Tunisian expatriates suspected of ties to Al Qaeda have been arrested in Afghanistan, Pakistan, Iraq, Western Europe, Mauritania, and the United States. Several are reportedly detained at the U.S. Naval Base in Guantanamo

Bay, Cuba, and their possible return to Tunisia has proven to be controversial.[32] In April 2009, General David Petraeus, then-Commander of U.S. Central Command, told a House Appropriations Committee subcommittee that the perpetrators of suicide bombings in Iraq that month may have been part of a network based in Tunisia.[33]

Under Ben Ali, as many as 2,000 Tunisians were detained, charged, and/or convicted on terrorism-related charges, including under a sweeping anti-terrorism law passed in 2003.[34] Critics claimed that the law "makes the exercise of fundamental freedoms ... an expression of terrorism."[35] These criticisms were echoed in the December 2010 report of the U.N. Special Rapporteur on the Promotion and Protection of Human Rights and Fundamental Freedoms While Countering Terrorism, who concluded that "the current definition of terrorism is vague and broad, hence deviating from the principle of legality and allowing for wide usage of counter-terrorism measures in practice."[36] Rights advocates also accused anti-terror trials of relying on excessive pretrial detention, denial of due process, and weak evidence. Current President Marzouki was a prominent critic of the former regime's anti-terrorism trials on human rights grounds. The government's approach to counterterrorism, and the status of the law, have yet to be seen amid broader efforts to continue political and civil liberties reforms and to restructure the judiciary.

SELECTED PROFILES

- **Hamadi Jebali, Prime Minister and Secretary-General of Al Nahda.** Born 1949 in Sousse, Jebali is an engineer and a longtime Al Nahda activist, having served in the group's political bureau in 1981 and as its president from 1981 until 1984. He also directed Al Nahda's newspaper, *Al Fajr*. In 1992, Jebali was sentenced to 16 years in prison in a mass trial of Al Nahda members. He spent 10 years in solitary confinement. Previously, Jebali lived for 10 years in France, where he completed an engineering degree and was a founder of the French Muslim Association. Jebali has rejected the label "Islamist"—maintaining that Al Nahda is a "civil political party"—and is viewed by some observers as the "moderate" or "reformist" face of the party.[37]
- **Moncef Marzouki, President and Leader of the Congress for the Republic (CPR).** Born in 1945, Marzouki is a medical doctor, author,

and longtime human rights activist. After medical school in France, he taught medicine at the University of Sousse from 1981 to 2000, while increasingly becoming a leader in national and regional human rights advocacy. He was jailed several times for his activism and for attempting to run for president against Ben Ali. In 2001, Marzouki founded the left-leaning, secularist CPR party on a platform of establishing the rule of law and promoting human rights. It was banned, leading Marzouki to a decade of exile and diaspora activism in France. While outside the country and during the electoral campaign, Marzouki signaled that he was willing to forge common cause with Islamists, at times criticizing more stringent secularists for being out of touch with ordinary Tunisians.[38]

- **Mustapha Ben Jaafar, President of the Constituent Assembly and Leader of Ettakatol.** Ben Jaafar, 71, founded the center-left, secularist Ettakatol (alt: Democratic Forum for Labor and Liberties, or FDTL) party in 1994. It eventually became one of three "dissident" opposition parties recognized under Ben Ali, which operated under significant restrictions. Ben Jaafar tried to run for president in 2009 but the government rejected his candidacy. A medical doctor trained in France, Ben Jaafar became engaged in political and human rights activism in the 1970s, while serving on the medical faculty at the University of Tunis.
- **Maya Jribi, leader of the Progressive Democratic Party (PDP) and of the Constituent Assembly secularist opposition.** Jribi, 52, became the first female secretary-general of a political party in 2006 when she assumed the PDP leadership. Both Jribi and the PDP's founder, Ahmed Najib Chebbi, won seats in the National Constituent Assembly. A biologist by training and the first woman to lead a major political party, Jribi has positioned herself as leader of the secularist parliamentary opposition. Founded in the 1980s, the PDP (like Ettakatol) was one of a small handful of legal but repressed opposition parties under Ben Ali.
- **Rachid Ghannouchi, President and Co-Founder of Al Nahda.** An Islamic scholar, teacher, and activist, Ghannouchi, 71, has led Tunisia's main Islamist movement for three decades but has no formal role in the current government. Ghannouchi's early focus was on religious and moral issues, but he grew more politically active by the late 1970s. He spent two decades in exile, largely in London, after Al Nahda was banned in 1991, returning to Tunisia in January 2011 upon

the announcement of a general amnesty. Ghannouchi has emphasized that Al Nahda seeks to participate within a democratic system and that the party will not attempt to turn back women's rights or other liberal aspects of Tunisian society. However, Tunisian secularists view him and his party with suspicion. Ghannouchi has stated that he will soon step down from the leadership of the party and is not interested in running for president.

Background on Tunisia's Trade Unions

Since Tunisia's independence, the labor movement has served as a rare legal conduit for expressing dissent, and the largest (and previously sole legal) union federation, the Tunisian General Union of Labor (UGTT), wields significant political clout. The UGTT, which claims over half a million members, played a key role in sustaining the 2011 protest movement, which it framed as rooted in economic grievances. The UGTT suffered from internal fracturing in the aftermath of Ben Ali's departure, but since early 2012 has sought to reposition itself as a key counterweight to Al Nahda. New unions and splinter movements have recently been formed, which may compete with the UGTT for influence. UGTT activists formed candidate lists in the October 2011 election under the banner of the Tunisian Labor Party (PTT), but did not win any seats.

The UGTT was organized in the mid-1940s and was a force in Tunisia's independence movement. During the Cold War, it positioned itself as pro-West (non-Communist) and formed links with the American labor movement.[39] Tunisia's first president, Habib Bourguiba, strove to keep the unions under the government's wing; during the 1960s, former UGTT leader Ahmed Ben Salah led a decade-long period of socialist-oriented economic policy as minister for finance and planning. By the late 1970s and into the mid-1980s, however, amid growing economic unease, the union's leadership turned to overt confrontation with the government, particularly over wages and food price inflation.[40] The UGTT led a series of strikes and demonstrations that were met with heavy state repression. During Ben Ali's presidency, the government again attempted to influence the UGTT, including by interfering in its leadership selection. The UGTT nevertheless was a key instigator of anti-government unrest in recent years, including protests in the mining region of Gafsa in 2008 and 2010 that were arguably a precursor to the "Jasmine Revolution" uprising.

The Economy

For many Tunisians, the 2011 uprising was motivated by socioeconomic grievances as much as a desire for political change. Some observers therefore fear that a failure to deliver rapid economic benefits could lead an impatient public to lose faith in the transition process. Indeed, the economic situation has worsened since 2011 due to perceived political uncertainty, turmoil in neighboring Libya, and the debt crisis in the European Union, which is Tunisia's largest trading partner. Declines in tourism and foreign direct investment (FDI) have been particularly damaging. The economy contracted by 1.8% in 2011, compared to growth of 3.7% in 2010; unemployment rose from 13% in 2010 to above 18% as of early 2012.[41] In October 2011, the International Monetary Fund (IMF) projected that the worsening global economic outlook would negatively impact Tunisia's growth prospects in 2012, and warned of widening fiscal deficits.[42] Tunisia's credit ratings have been repeatedly downgraded. Still, international economic policymakers are optimistic about the country's medium-term prospects,[43] and this year has seen a slight rebound in both growth and FDI.[44]

Most Tunisian politicians have embraced broad free-market principles while advocating state-led efforts to reduce economic and regional inequality. Tunisian officials have pursued fiscally expansive policies in an effort to boost employment and have appealed for outside financial support to provide emergency relief before long-term reforms can be put in place. The government recently threatened to remove the governor of the Central Bank, Kamel Nabli, who has broad international support, following disputes over who has the authority to set monetary policy—in particular, the target for inflation, which may be affected by fiscal expansion.[45]

Tunisia is considered a middle-income country, and prior to 2011 had been one of the best-performing non-oil-exporting Arab countries. Home and car ownership are widespread. Textile exports and tourism have driven much of Tunisia's economic growth in recent years. Tunisia has also attempted to attract foreign investment in its nascent oil and gas sector. Phosphate ore reserves are significant and are the basis of a chemicals industry. However, Tunisia's strong economic record long masked significant disparities and structural problems. Wealth is concentrated in the capital and along the eastern coast, while the interior has suffered from poverty and a lack of investment. Tunisians are among the most educated people in North Africa, but the economy has generally created low-skilled and low-paid jobs. Unemployment and underemployment are major problems, notably for recent college graduates. Unemployment is highest in interior regions, such as Kasserine and Gafsa, which were epicenters of the revolution and which continue to see protests over perceived government neglect.[46]

Recovery of State Assets

Ben Ali and Trabelsi family members owned or controlled many of the country's biggest companies, with shares sometimes allegedly obtained through political pressure or corruption, and are thought to have stashed away significant assets overseas. Tunisian authorities have identified at least 12 countries where these individuals stored money, which could total billions of dollars. Western governments have cooperated with Tunisian efforts to freeze assets; however, the process for recovering them on behalf of the Tunisian state is complex and challenging.[47]

In early 2011, authorities seized shares of domestic companies controlled by Ben Ali family members and close associates accused of financial manipulation. The list of assets touched upon every major economic sector and included some of Tunisia's largest companies. It is unclear what percentages of shares in each company were appropriated by the state, but the total value may amount to $2 billion.[48] The companies have continued to operate under state-appointed managers; how the frozen assets are handled in the future may be determined by the courts.

Foreign Relations

Al Nahda officials and other political leaders have emphasized continuity in Tunisia's foreign relations, for instance regarding international agreements made under Ben Ali. They have also stated that they wish to protect and expand foreign direct investment and international trade, including with traditional partners in the West. The party has simultaneously indicated a desire to cultivate closer political and economic ties to other Arab and Muslim states, and to Sub-Saharan Africa.[49]

In particular, relations with Arab Gulf states and with Turkey—which have offered aid and public support to the current government—appear set to grow closer. The Tunisian government is supportive of Syrian opposition forces, hosting a Syrian National Council meeting in December 2011 and the first international "Friends of Syria" meeting in February 2012.

Israel and the Palestinians

Tunisians broadly sympathize with the Palestinians; Tunisia hosted the Palestine Liberation Organization (PLO) headquarters in exile from 1982 to 1993. Tunisia had an interests office in Israel from 1996 until the outbreak of the second Palestinian *intifadah*, or uprising against the Israeli occupation of the West Bank and Gaza Strip, in 2000; under Ben Ali, Israeli and Tunisian foreign ministers sometimes met. Al Nahda leader Ghannouchi refers to Israel as an "occupying state," and has indicated that the creation of a Palestinian state is a prerequisite for discussing Tunisian-Israeli ties.[50] The government has hosted two visits by senior Hamas officials, as well as a visit by Palestinian Authority President Mahmoud Abbas. Al Nahda's position on Israel and the Palestinians does not appear to be very different from other political parties in Tunisia. Tunisia's then-interim Foreign Ministry—led at the time by secularists—announced in September 2011 that it would support the Palestinians' bid for U.N. recognition of statehood. Indeed, some domestic critics have accused Al Nahda of being too conciliatory toward Israel.[51]

Europe

Tunisia and the European Union (EU) have cemented a close relationship by means of an Association Agreement, aid, and loans.[52] More than 62% of Tunisia's trade is conducted with Europe.[53] The Association Agreement, which was signed in 1995 and entered into force in 1998, eliminates customs tariffs and other trade barriers on manufactured goods, and provides for the establishment of an EU-Tunisia free trade area in goods, but not in agriculture or services. The EU has focused high-level attention on Tunisia's political transition, providing additional aid and technical cooperation, and re-starting negotiations on the provision of "advanced status" for Tunisia, which would provide greater trade benefits.[54] Debt relief is also a possibility.[55] Europeans hope that aid will help Tunisia's growth and thereby reduce illegal immigration, and that the promise of greater economic integration will incentivize democracy and human rights.

Relations with France were strained over French support for Ben Ali, which was extended even as his security forces cracked down on pro-democracy protesters. France, the former colonial power, had cultivated close ties with the Ben Ali regime, which it saw as ensuring regional stability and a destination for French investment. French authorities have sought to ingratiate themselves with post-Ben Ali authorities by replacing their ambassador, imposing an asset freeze on Ben Ali family members and associates, dispatching senior officials on state visits, and pledging new aid.[56] French officials congratulated Al Nahda on its election victory, but later than other donors; suspicion of Islamists persists in French political circles.

Regional Relations

Tunisia has generally sought cordial relations with its immediate neighbors, although Ben Ali's entente with neighboring Libya's Muammar al Qadhafi was strained. Although it declined to participate militarily in U.S. and NATO military operations in Libya, Tunisia has been strongly supportive of the transition there, and recognized Libya's Transitional National Council (TNC) on August 21, 2011. Tunisian authorities hope that an end to turmoil in Libya will stabilize border areas and, eventually, produce an economic rebound that would allow Libya to reabsorb some of Tunisia's low-skilled labor surplus. In December 2011, Al Nahda leader Ghannouchi participated in a TNC-led Libyan reconciliation and reconstruction forum.

Algeria and Morocco have been publicly supportive of Tunisia's transition: Algeria has offered financial assistance, while Morocco and Tunisia signed a bilateral military cooperation agreement in May 2011. President Marzouki has led a high-profile campaign to revitalize the Arab Maghreb Union, which was established in 1989 by Tunisia, Algeria, Morocco, Libya, and Mauritania, but has been long inactive due to tensions between Morocco and Algeria. Tunis is also the temporary headquarters location of the African Development Bank (AfDB), which receives significant financial support from the United States; it moved to Tunisia in 2005 due to unrest in Côte d'Ivoire, its permanent location.

U.S.-Tunisian Relations

During Ben Ali's presidency, the United States balanced deep and persistent concerns about political repression, corruption, and human rights abuses with a desire to cooperate with Tunisia's government on counterterrorism and regional security. Administration officials have since emphasized strong support for Tunisia's democratic transition, as well as a desire to advance bilateral economic ties and enhance cooperation on regional policy concerns such as the crisis in Syria and economic integration in the Maghreb. In a speech in May 2011 on U.S. policy toward the Middle East, President Obama called on the United States "to show that America values the dignity of the street vendor in Tunisia more than the raw power of the dictator."[57] In February 2012, Secretary of State Hillary Clinton visited Tunis and stated that she was "a very strong champion for Tunisian democracy and what has been accomplished here," adding, "the challenge is how to ensure the economic development of Tunisia matches the political development."[58]

Then-Interim Prime Minister Caïd Essebsi met with President Obama at the White House in October 2011, and President Obama called Prime Minister Jebali in December 2011 to congratulate him on his appointment.[59] Al Nahda president Rachid Ghannouchi—who does not hold a formal government position—visited Washington, DC, in November 2011, but did not make a public appearance with U.S. officials. In May 2011, prior to the elections and his appointment as prime minister, Hamadi Jebali visited Washington on the invitation of a private organization. On the Tunisian side, priorities appear to include U.S. economic and military aid, U.S. technical and diplomatic support for recovering frozen assets linked to the former regime, and the return of Tunisian nationals detained at the U.S. Naval Base in Guantanamo Bay, among other issues. The Administration has indicated that, with regard to working with regional Islamist actors such as Al Nahda, "what parties call themselves is less important to us than what they actually do."[60] This principle may be tested in the months ahead as Tunisia's coalition government seeks a vay forward on complex domestic and foreign policy dilemmas.[61]

In February 2012, Secretary of State Clinton expressed support for tiations toward a free trade agreement (FTA) with Tunisia in testimony Congress.[62] Any progress on an FTA would be subject to an ıcy process, among other factors. U.S.-Tunisian trade is currently limited: in 2011, U.S. bilateral exports totaled $586 million and ed $352 million.[63] Tunisia is eligible for certain trade preferences eralized System of Preferences (GSP) Program. A bilateral trade ework agreement (TIFA) was signed in 2002, and a bilateral entered into force in 1993. TIFAs can be the first step toward

ations date back over 200 years. Tunisia was the site of g World War II, and was liberated by Allied forces in A U.S. cemetery and memorial near the ancient city holds nearly 3,000 U.S. military dead. During the a pro-Western foreign policy despite a brief

stance
, U.S.
highly

experiment with leftist economic policy in the 1960s. Still, U.S.-Tunisian ties were strained by the 1985 Israeli bombing of the Palestinian Liberation Organization headquarters in Tunis, which some viewed as having been carried out with U.S. approval.[64] Tunisia cooperates in NATO's Operation Active Endeavor, which provides counterterrorism surveillance in the Mediterranean; participates in NATO's Mediterranean Dialogue; and allows NATO ships to make port calls at Tunis.

U.S. Foreign Assistance

Congress authorizes, appropriates, and oversees foreign ass funding, and regularly authorizes arms sale proposals. Prior to 201 bilateral aid to Tunisia was modest by regional standards and wa focused on security cooperation. Tunisia has hosted the regional office of the State Department's Middle East Partnership Initiative (MEPI) since 2004, but had not previously received significant funds; in FY2010, Tunisia received $21.9 million in bilateral aid, of which $20.2 million was security assistance. The Obama Administration has since offered a range of new foreign assistance aimed broadly at "transition support," as well as a reinvigoration of the trade relationship (see above). The State Department has allocated over $300 million in bilateral transition aid (broadly defined) and security assistance to Tunisia since early 2011.[68] Aid funding has drawn on monies appropriated in FY2010-FY2012, much of it reprogrammed from other sources. Non-security aid is focused on civil society, political parties, the independent media, election support, youth and women participation, and economic reforms. It includes two programs authorized in P.L. 112-74, the FY2012 Consolidated Appropriations Act:

- $30 million for the cost of sovereign loan guarantees, which are expected to enable Tunisia to raise some $400 million on the international bond market;[69] and
- $20 million for the creation of a bilateral "Enterprise Fund" designed to spur private investment and encourage economic reforms.

The transition aid allocation also includes $100 million that is being provided as a cash transfer to the Tunisian government for short-term fiscal relief, as notified to Congress in April 2012.[70] An additional Millennium Challenge "threshold" grant worth about $20 million is anticipated; a Peace Corps program is also being re-established. U.S.-funded democracy assistance organizations have not, to date, been the targets of official harassment as they have in Egypt. Still, commentary published in the local press has highlighted public debates regarding the basis and impact of U.S. democracy aid, and over whether such aid constitutes foreign interference.[71]

The Administration has requested $36.6 million in total bilateral aid for FY2013;[72] however, Tunisia is likely to receive much more in funding directed from regional allocations, reprogrammed funds, and other sources. The State Department's Office for Middle East Transitions, established in September 2011 and led by Ambassador William Taylor, is administering a Middle East Response Fund/Middle East and North Africa Incentive Fund (MERF/MENA-IF) constituted from unobligated FY2011 and FY2012 Economic Support Fund (ESF) funding. The Office and Congress have identified an initial $185 million for the MERF, including $50 million identified in the conference report on P.L. 112-74. Tunisia has been the main beneficiary to date, with $71.2 million allocated as of early 2012. The Obama Administration is requesting a further $770 million for the MENA-IF in FY2013. In addition to bilateral assistance, the Overseas Private Investment Corporation (OPIC) is "working to invest" roughly $150 million in Tunisia.[73]

Multilateral financial institutions that receive U.S. financial support have also pledged significant aid. The United States has been supportive of efforts by the Group of Eight (G8)—under the banner of the 2011 "Deauville Partnership"—and by the European Bank for Reconstruction and Development to provide aid to Tunisia and other countries affected by the "Arab Spring."[74]

Security cooperation appears likely to increase due to interest on both sides. A Joint Military Commission meets annually and joint exercises are held regularly. Tunisia relies on U.S. Foreign Military Financing (FMF) assistance and Foreign Military Sales (FMS) agreements to maintain its aging inventory of U.S.-origin equipment, and the Tunisian military views International Military Education and Training (IMET) as a key tool for officer training. Tunisia is set to receive $29.5 million in FMF and $1.9 million in IMET in FY2012;[75] the Administration has requested $15 million and $2.3 million, respectively, for FY2013. The Administration has also requested $8 million in FY2013 International Narcotics Control and Law Enforcement (INCLE) funding for police and justice sector assistance. The Administration allocated $13 million in Defense Department-administered "Section 1206" funding for a maritime and border security package in FY2011.[76] Tunisia is also among 10 countries participating in the U.S. Trans-Sahara Counter-Terrorism Partnership (TSCTP), an interagency regional program that aims to enhance capacity and cooperation on security issues in North and West Africa.

OUTLOOK

Recent events, including political contestation and unrest across the Middle East and North Africa, raise potential issues for Congress pertaining to the oversight of U.S.-Tunisian bilateral relations, foreign assistance, and broader U.S. policy priorities in the Middle East. Possible questions include the following:

- To what extent is Tunisia a "test-case" for democratic transitions in the Middle East? To what extent is Tunisia a priority for U.S. policy in the region? What are the prospects for U.S. influence on the future evolution of events in Tunisia? How should the United States shape its future foreign aid programs? What course of U.S. action is most likely to fulfill foreign policy and national security goals?

- What are the key issues in constitution drafting, and how will Tunisians seek to overcome differences in key policy preferences? What type of political system will emerge in Tunisia? Will the new constitution protect individual rights and ensure equality for religious, ethnic, and political minorities?
- Do continued protests and border insecurity constitute significant threats? Do elements of the former regime continue to influence events in Tunisia? How will transitional authorities approach the question of reforming the internal security services and providing for transitional justice?
- Which individuals and groups currently enjoy significant popular credibility in Tunisia? Which emergent coalitions among political and interest groups are likely to endure?
- What is the future trajectory of Tunisia's economy? What is the appropriate role of Tunisia's international partners in helping Tunisia to promote economic growth and job creation, and to address regional economic disparities?

End Notes

[1] The October 23, 2011, elections were widely viewed as fair, transparent, and well-conducted, despite earlier delays and preparations that often appeared disjointed. Participation in the historic vote prompted deep emotions among many voters, polling station workers, and domestic observers. Still, observers expressed concerns regarding the allocation of voters to polling stations; administrative difficulties encountered by voters who had not formally registered, most of whom were eligible to vote at special polling centers; limited voter education; and a lack of detailed procedures and training for key parts of the process. Many Tunisians appeared to feel alienated by the complexity of the transition process and a lack of understanding of the Constituent Assembly's role.

[2] See International Crisis Group (ICG), *Tunisia: Combating Impunity, Restoring Security*, May 9, 2012.

[3] The independent commission that oversaw the October 2011 elections, known as the ISIE, has been dissolved pending decisions on how to organize the next electoral process, and the future status of the electoral law is uncertain.

[4] Duncan Pickard, "The Current Status of Constitution Making in Tunisia," Carnegie Endowment, April 19, 2012.

[5] ICG, *Tunisia: Confronting Social and Economic Challenges*, June 6, 2012.

[6] See CRS Report R42393, *Change in the Middle East: Implications for U.S. Policy*, coordinated by Christopher M. Blanchard.

[7] Tunisia's spending on education (7.2% of gross domestic product) is high by regional standards. CIA, *The World Factbook*, updated January 3, 2011.

[8] EIU, *Tunisia: Country Profile*, 2008.

[9] *Associated Press* (*AP*), "Report Raises Number of Killed During Tunisia's Revolution to 338," May 5, 2012.

[10] Ghannouchi remains president of the party, although he does not hold a position in government. Mourou has left the party and was an (unsuccessful) independent candidate in the October elections.

[11] The system of proportional representation adopted for the October elections was designed to preclude any single party from easily gaining a majority. This resulted in parties such as the CPR, the PDP, and Ettakatol gaining a larger proportion of seats than votes.

[12] E.g., *African Manager*, "Tunisie: Ressemblances surprenantes, Ben Ali-RCD & Jbali-Ennahdha," February 27, 2012.

[13] Earlier, Al Nahda leader Ghannouchi had suggested the party had yet to reach an internal consensus on the issue. Walid Khefifi, "Rached Ghannouchi, président du mouvement islamiste Ennahdha: 'Le recours à une intervention militaire ne sera pas au menu de la conférence des amis de la Syrie,'" *Le Temps*, February 24, 2012 ; Kareem Fahim, "Tunisia Says Constitution Will Not Cite Islamic Law," *The New York Times*, March 26, 2012 ; AFP, "Tunisie/Charia: Ennahda a 'levé l'ambiguité', se félicitent des modernistes," March 27, 2012.

[14] "Salafism" refers to a broad subset of Sunni revivalist movements that seek to purify contemporary Islamic religious practices and societies by encouraging the application of practices and views associated with the earliest days of the Islamic faith. Salafist movements hold a range of positions on political, social, and theological questions and include both politically quietist and violent extremist groups. See CRS Report RS21745, *Islam: Sunnis and Shiites*, by Christopher M. Blanchard.

[15] For example, In February 2012, the government announced the arrest of 12 people linked to a violent Salafist cell and the seizure of an arms depot, near the commercial city of Sfax. Soon afterward, the government delivered the first ever political party license to a Salafist group.

[16] Reportedly, the exhibit featured a work in which the word "Allah" was displayed in the form of insects.

[17] *AP*, "Minister Warns Tunisia's Patience Is at an End After Hardline Islamist Violence," May 31, 2012; *AFP*, "Tunisia on Edge After Night of 'Terrorist' Attacks," June 12, 2012.

[18] Henry Munson Jr., "Islamic Revivalism in Morocco and Tunisia," *The Muslim World*, 76:3-4 (1986).

[19] Christopher Alexander, *Tunisia: Stability and Reform in the Modern Maghreb*, Routledge: New York, 2010.

[20] Hamadi Redissi, "The Revolution Is Not Over Yet [op-ed]," *The New York Times*, July 15, 2011; Tarek Amara, "Tunisia Pledges Tougher Line on Ex-Leader's Allies," *Reuters*, August 18, 2011; ICG, "Combating Impunity," op. cit.

[21] See, e.g., Richard Cochrane, "Dismissal of Security Chief Sparks Coup Rumors in Tunisia," IHS Global Analysis, January 12, 2012; and France24.com, "Leaked Video: 'The Return of Ben Ali's Porno-Politics,'" January 20, 2012.

[22] *Reuters*, "Smuggling Stirs Trouble on Tunisia's Libya Border," May 2, 2012.

[23] Aaron Y. Zelin, "Tarek Maaroufi: Tunisia's Most Notorious Jihadist, Returns Home," *Tunisia Live*, April 1, 2012.

[24] OSC doc. GMP20110128836001, "AQLIM Warns Tunisians Against Western 'Plots' To 'Abort' Tunisian Revolution," Al-Mujahidin Electronic Network, January 28, 2011. For background on AQIM, see CRS Report R41070, *Al Qaeda and Affiliates: Historical Perspective, Global Presence, and Implications for U.S. Policy*, coordinated by John Rollins.

[25] Radio Tunisienne, "Tunisian Interior Ministry Provides More Information on 'Terrorists' Arrest," May 16, 2011, via U.S. government Open Source Center (OSC); BBC Monitoring, "Militants From Al-Qa'idah Try to Sneak into Tunisia, Official," July 2, 2011; *AFP*, "Six Killed in Tunisian Clashes Near Algeria: Diplomat," September 23, 2011; *AP*, "Armed Cell Is Tied to Al Qaeda, Official Says, as 12 Members Are Held," February 13, 2012.

[26] Maamoun Youssef, "Al-Qaida's No. 2 Incites Tunisians, Egyptians," *AP*, February 28, 2011; OSC doc. GMP20110913836004, "Al-Fajr Releases Al-Zawahiri Audio, Bin Ladin Video on 10th Anniversary of 9/11," Ana Al Muslim Network, September 13, 2011; *AP*, "Ayman al Zawahri, Al Qaeda Leader, Incites Tunisians Against Ruling Party," June 10, 2012.

[27] *Middle East Online*, "Gannouchi Describes Zawahiri as 'Disaster for Islam and Muslims,'" June 13, 2012.

[28] Recent news reports, based on purported revelations by former security officers, have alleged that there was an incipient plot by the internal security services to take power upon Ben Ali's departure in January 2011, which was foiled when the military refused to go along. See, e.g., *Financial Times*, "Ben Ali Feared Betrayal by Inner Circle," January 12, 2012.

[29] Issandr El Amrani, "Tunisia Diary: Ammar's Move?" *TheArabist.net*, January 24, 2011. In mid-2010, an analysis of Tunisia's political stability concluded that "a coup is a real possibility" should instability affect the transfer of power after Ben Ali. Veritiss, *Tunisia: Outlook 2011-2015* [UNCLASSIFIED], prepared For the Defense Intelligence Agency Defense Intelligence Open Source Program Office, August 2, 2010.

[30] *Financial Times*, "Al-Qaeda Deputy Leader Signals Involvement in Attacks," October 10, 2002.

[31] U.S. State Department, *Country Reports on Terrorism, 2006*, April 30, 2007. The TCG is no longer so designated.

[32] According to news reports, 12 Tunisians were at one time detained in Guatanamo, but only five remain in U.S. custody. Five were repatriated to third countries, partly due to concerns over their possible torture if returned to Tunisia, while two others were returned to Tunisia and imprisoned. Bouazza Ben Bouazza, "Tunisia to Send Mission to US for Release of its Remaining Gitmo Detainees," September 14, 2011.

[33] *House Appropriations Subcommittee on Military Construction, Veterans Affairs, and Related Agencies Holds Hearing on the US Central Command*, April 24, 2009, transcript via *CQ*.

[34] U.S. State Department, *Country Reports on Terrorism, 2009*, released August 5, 2010.

[35] Jeremy Landor, "Washington's Partner," *Middle East International*, March 5, 2004, pp. 23-24.

[36] U.N. Human Rights Council, *Report of the Special Rapporteur*, December 28, 2010, op. cit.

[37] "Profile: Tunisian Ennahdha Prime Minister Candidate Hammadi Jebali," via OSC, October 28, 2011; *Al Arabiya*, "Tunisia's Hamadi Jebali: The Face of Moderate Islam?" November 18, 2011.

[38] *LePoint.fr*, "L'Opposant Historique Moncef Marzouki Va Devenir Président," November 21, 2011.

[39] Global Security, "Union Génerale des Travailleurs Tunisiens (UGTT)," at http://www.global security.org /military/ world/tunisia/ugtt.htm.

[40] See Niger Disney, "The Working-Class Revolt in Tunisia," Middle East Research and Information Project (MERIP) Reports, 67 (May 1978).

[41] *Bloomberg*, "Arab Spring Turns to Economic Winter on More Joblessness," March 27, 2012.

[42] *IMF Survey*, "Mideast Outlook Varies Markedly Across Regions," October 26, 2011. IMF Managing Director Christine Lagarde echoed this analysis during a visit to Tunis; see IMF press release No. 12/32, February 2, 2012.

[43] CRS interviews with World Bank officials working on the North Africa region, January 2012.

[44] *Reuters*, "Tunisia's Economy Returns to Growth in Q1 2012," May 24, 2012; *TAP*, "TIF [Tunisia Investment Forum] 2012 Opens," June 14, 2012.

[45] *Reuters*, "Tunisia Govt To Propose Firing Central Bank Governor," May 27, 2012.

[46] African Development Bank, *The Revolution in Tunisia: Economic Challenges and Prospects*, March 2011.

[47] Deborah Ball and Cassell Bryan-Low, "Arab Spring Regimes Face Long Slog to Recoup Assets," *The Wall Street Journal*, August 25, 2011; Robert F. Worth, "Obstacles Mar Quest for Arab Dictators' Assets," *The New York Times*, June 7, 2012. U.S. investigators reportedly opened a preliminary probe into assets controlled by Ben Ali and family members in early 2011.

[48] State Department, "2012 Investment Climate Statement – Tunisia," June 2012.

[49] CRS interviews with Rachid Ghannouchi and Hamadi Jebali, Tunis, October 2011; *AFP*, "La Tunisie de l'après Ben Ali veut retrouver toute sa place en Afrique," January 29, 2012.

[50] CRS interviews with Rachid Ghannouchi and Hamadi Jebali, Tunis, October 2011; and Ghannouchi statements at the Project on Middle East Democracy (POMED), November 30, 2011.

[51] E.g., Al Jazeera, "Calls for Tunisia to Criminalize Normalization of Ties with Israel," December 31, 2011, via BBC Monitoring Middle East.

[52] At the same time, EU leaders periodically expressed concerns over Tunisia's record on human rights and political freedom under Ben Ali.

[53] World Trade Organization, *Tunisia Profile*, October 2011.

[54] See European Commission, EuropeAid Development and Cooperation, *Tunisia*, at http://ec.europa.eu/europeaid/where/neighbourhood/country-cooperation/tunisia /tunisia_en.htm.

[55] *AFP*, "EU Opens Door to 'Debt Relief' for North African States," February 22, 2012.

[56] See G8 Summit, "The Deauville Partnership: Helping the Arab Countries in Their Transition to Free and Democratic Societies," Deauville, May 27, 2011.

[57] The White House, "Remarks by the President on the Middle East and Africa," May 19, 2011.

[58] State Department, "Secretary of State Clinton Delivers Remarks Following Meeting with Tunisia President Marzouki," February 25, 2012.

[59] White House, "Readout of the President's Call with Tunisian Interim Prime Minister Jebali," December 19, 2011.

[60] Bradley Klapper, "Championing Democracy, Clinton Says US Can Work with Islamist Parties Gaining from Arab Spring," November 8, 2011.

[61] For example, in May 2012, the U.S. ambassador to Tunisia stated that he was "disappointed" by a television station owner's blasphemy conviction; the government responded that his remarks constituted "interference in Tunisian justice." *La Presse*, "Le ministère des A.E. proteste contre les déclarations de l'ambassadeur US," May 9, 2012.

[62] Secretary of State Hillary Clinton, testimony before the Senate Appropriations Committee, Subcommittee on State, Foreign Operations, and Related Programs, February 28, 2012, transcript via *Congressional Quarterly* (*CQ*).

[63] U.S. International Trade Commission data, accessed at http://dataweb.usitc.gov/.

[64] Chicago Tribune Wires, "Bush Visits Tunisia to Patch Relations," March 9, 1986; Jonathan C. Randal, "Raid Left Scars on U.S.-Tunisia Ties," *The Washington Post*, March 5, 1987.

[65] *AFP*, "US Concerned About Reports of 'Excessive Force' in Tunisia," January 11, 2011; and U.S. State Department, "Secretary of State Interviewed on Al Arabiya," January 11, 2011, via *CQ*.

[66] The White House, "Statement by the President on Events in Tunisia," January 14, 2011.

[67] Testimony of Director of National Intelligence James Clapper, House Select Intelligence Committee Hearing on Worldwide Threats, February 10, 2011, via *CQ*.

[68] State Department response to CRS inquiry, May 2012.

[69] See State Department, "U.S. Loan Guarantee Supports Tunisia's Democratic Transition," June 11, 2012.

[70] The transfer will fund payments on debt that Tunisia owes the World Bank and African Development Bank. According to the State Department, this will allow the government "to instead use this money for its priority programs, accelerating economic growth and job creation." Secretary of State Clinton, "Assistance to Tunisia," March 29, 2012. The transfer will be paid for in FY2012 Economic Support Fund (ESF) funding originally appropriated for Overseas Contingency Operations under the International Counter-Narcotics and Law Enforcement heading. U.S. Agency for International Development (USAID), congressional notification #39, April 11, 2012.

[71] See, e.g., Asma Ghribi, "State Department Program's Funding of Tunisian Media Comes Under Scrutiny," *Tunisia Live*, January 20, 2012.

[72] State Department, FY2013 *Congressional Budget Justification, Foreign Operations*.

[73] State Department, "Tunisia: Overview of U.S. Economic Assistance," February 25, 2012.

[74] Fact-sheets on these multilateral initiatives can be found at http://www.state.gov /r/pa/prs/ps/2012/05/190516.htm (May 21, 2012).

[75] State Department response to CRS inquiry, May 2012.

[76] The 1206 package was initially notified to Congress at $20 million but not all of it was obligated as planned. For more information on Section 1206 funding, see CRS Report RS22855, *Security Assistance Reform: "Section 1206" Background and Issues for Congress*, by Nina M. Serafino.

In: Tunisia: Transition and Challenges
Editors: H. Sanchez and R. Freeman
ISBN: 978-1-62417-755-2

Chapter 2

The Prospects for Security Sector Reform in Tunisia: A Year after the Revolution*

Querine Hanlon

Foreword

The Arab Spring began in Tunisia. The tragic self-immolation of Mohammed Bouazizi in December 2010 struck a chord of discontent and frustration that ultimately propelled Tunisian President Zine El Abidine Ben Ali to step down barely a month later. The reverberations of this unprecedented series of events were felt throughout the region, and protestors took to the streets in Bahrain, Egypt, Libya, Morocco, Syria, and Yemen. A year later, Tunisia's remarkable transition continues to influence the region.

Tunisia has achieved in 1 year what none of the other Arab Spring states have been able to accomplish. Some have suggested that Tunisia's transition might even be a model for the Arab Spring countries. The Tunisian military's refusal to fire on the demonstrators and its decision to eschew an overtly political role in the transition have left the task of creating a new political order in Tunisia to the civilian bureaucracy, nascent political parties, and civil society groups. In national elections widely heralded to be free and fair,

---

* This is an edited, reformatted and augmented version of Strategic Studies Institute Publication, dated September 2012.

Tunisians elected a caretaker government and a National Constituent Assembly charged with drafting a new constitution for Tunisia in 2012.

In this chapter, Dr. Querine Hanlon of the National Defense University and the United States Institute of Peace finds that Tunisia is well poised to undertake serious security sector reform (SSR). SSR is a comprehensive tool for fixing the dysfunctional security sectors in fragile states emerging from conflict, developing capacities to meet the human security needs of their populations, or transitioning from authoritarian rule. In many fragile states, the security institutions are themselves a major source of insecurity. Dr. Hanlon argues that transforming the security sector into one that is democratically accountable and functions in accordance with the rule of law is an important step toward averting the recurrence of insecurity and conflict and preventing newly democratic or transitioning regimes from reverting to authoritarian rule.

Although the prospects for SSR in Tunisia are perhaps better than in any other Middle East and North Africa (MENA) state following the Arab Spring, substantial challenges remain. Dr. Hanlon argues that the *raison d'être* of Ben Ali's security institutions was to protect the regime, not the population. The abuses of Tunisia's internal security institutions and the impunity with which they acted against ordinary citizens served as a catalyst for the protests that ended Ben Ali's rule. Reforming or otherwise dismantling this large and complex sector will be no easy task. The transition to democratic rule will require a fundamental reorientation of the mandate and institutional culture of the labyrinth of security institutions that constitute the Tunisian security sector. SSR will be critical for building trust in the government and its security institutions and central to the construct of a national narrative that undergirds a new social contract between the people of Tunisia and its government.

The Strategic Studies Institute is pleased to offer this chapter as part of the ongoing debate on the role of SSR in transforming the security sectors in the transitioning Arab Spring countries in accordance with democratic principles and the rule of law.

Douglas C. Lovelace, Jr.
Director, Strategic Studies Institute

About the Author

QUERINE HANLON is the National Defense University Senior Fellow at the United States Institute of Peace (USIP). Dr. Hanlon is currently on sabbatical from her appointment as Dean of Academic Affairs at the College of International Security Affairs, National Defense University (NDU). At USIP, Dr. Hanlon, with Dr. Richard Shultz of The Fletcher School, is conducting a major research project entitled, "Designing Security Sector Reform for the 21st Century." Dr. Hanlon is also working on security sector reform in North Africa and recently traveled to the region on a USIP engagement trip. At the National Defense University, Dr. Hanlon was instrumental in designing the College's post-September 9, 2011-focused security studies curriculum. During her tenure, she transformed the institution from a small University component to NDU's newest degree-granting college, and negotiated, funded, and implemented NDU's first satellite campus at the John F. Kennedy Special Warfare Center and School in Fort Bragg, NC. Dr. Hanlon also expanded the College's International Counterterrorism Fellowship Program, a partnership capacity-building program into NDU's largest international graduate program with over 400 graduates from 85 partner nations. Dr. Hanlon is Associate Professor at the College of International Security Affairs. Previously, Dr. Hanlon was also a nonresident Fellow at the National Strategy Information Center, participating in two key projects on "Adapting America's Security Paradigm to a New Era: Conflict, Coalitions, and Capabilities in the Contemporary Security Environment" (2008-10) and "Teaching About Armed Groups and Irregular Warfare" (2006-08).

Dr. Hanlon's recent publications include "Security Sector Reform in Tunisia: A Year After the Jasmine Revolution," USIP Special Report No. 304 (March 2012); *Adapting America's Security Paradigm and Security Agenda* (Washington, DC: National Strategy Information Center, 2011), with Roy Godson, Richard Shultz, and Samantha Ravich; "The Sources of Instability in the 21st Century," Strategic Studies Quarterly, Vol. 5, No. 2 (Summer 2011), with Richard Shultz, Roy Godson, and Samantha Ravich; *The Three Images of Ethnic War* (Praeger Security International, 2009); *Armed Groups and Irregular Warfare: Adapting Professional Military Education* (Washington, DC: National Strategy Information Center, 2009) with Roy Godson and Richard H. Shultz, Jr.; and "Globalization and the Transformation of Armed Groups," in *Armed Groups: Studies in National Security, Counterterrorism and Counterinsurgency,* Jeffrey Norwitz, ed. (Naval War College Press, 2008). Dr. Hanlon is a graduate of the Edmund A. Walsh School of Foreign Service, Georgetown University, and holds an M.A.L.D. and Ph.D. from The Fletcher School, Tufts University.

Summary

In the year since the revolution, Tunisia has achieved what no other Arab Spring country has managed: peaceful transition to democratic rule through national elections widely viewed to be free and fair. The legacy of the previous regime, however, remains: a complete lack of transparency, no real parliamentary or government oversight, and largely unchanged rules of engagement and training. Tunisia's internal security services are feared by the population and are themselves fearful of fulfilling their basic policing tasks. The Tunisian Armed Forces clearly ascribe to the concept of civilian oversight of the military. Although they are currently fulfilling a number of internal security tasks, they have publicly stated their intention to return to the barracks when the police can resume responsibility for internal security. Security sector reform (SSR) will be critical for building trust in the new government and its security institutions. The *raison d'être* of Ben Ali's security institutions was to protect the regime, not the population. SSR is essential for reorienting the mandate and institutional culture of Tunisia's labyrinth of security institutions. Serious reform of the security sector is essential if Tunisia's transition to democratic rule is to succeed in the long term.

Introduction

Mohammed Bouazizi's altercation with a policewoman in the dusty town of Sidi Bouzid, Tunisia, on December 17, 2010, was ordinary in its arbitrariness, but extraordinary for what it sparked. After spitting in and slapping his face, a local policewoman confiscated Bouazizi's vegetable cart—and all its goods bought on credit—and in so doing threatened his livelihood and the sole means of support for his entire family. Bouazizi tried to appeal to the local municipal officials, but they refused to see him. With little education and no prospect of another job, the 26-year-old man set himself on fire in front of the municipal headquarters building.[1] He succumbed to his wounds in the hospital on January 4, 2011, 10 days before Tunisian President Zine El Abidine Ben Ali was forced to step down.

Bouazizi's tragic protest struck a chord of discontent and frustration that sparked public demonstrations throughout Tunisia. The initial demonstrations took place on the day of Bouazizi's self-immolation in Sidi Bouzid and by late December had spread to the nearby cities of Kasserine and Thala. On January

12, demonstrations began in the capital of Tunis. What had begun as an outpouring of frustration and protest over poor economic conditions, and particularly high youth unemployment, rapidly escalated into an unprecedented challenge to Ben Ali's 23-year rule.

The internal security services—the police and the National Guard—responded in force. While some protests were largely peaceful, others turned violent. Police opened fire on crowds and arrested protestors, journalists and opposition party members, lawyers, and rights advocates. But the police response failed to quell the protests. On January 13, Ben Ali made a last-ditch attempt to save his rule. On national television, he pledged to step down when his term ended in 2014, offered new parliamentary elections, and vowed to end state censorship. But with the carrot came the stick. He deployed the military to buttress the internal security forces and, on January 14, declared a state of emergency that prohibited gatherings of more than three people and authorized the use of force against any individuals who ignored the ban.

Then General Rachid Ammar, Chief of Staff of the Army, struck a mortal blow. He said "No." The military's refusal to fire on the demonstrators left Ben Ali with no means to quash the demonstrators forcibly, and he fled to Saudi Arabia that same day.[2] In the immediate aftermath of his departure, there were numerous reports of violence between the security services and rogue elements. Elsewhere the police fled, and the Army was deployed to maintain order on the streets—assuming the internal security tasks of securing the population, manning checkpoints, and protecting strategic sites and public buildings.[3] Unlike the case of Egypt, however, the Tunisian military chose to stay at the critical margins. In a rare public address on January 24, General Ammar promised to uphold Tunisia's revolution and to guarantee stability until elections were held.[4] The military's critical decision to eschew an overtly political role in the transition left the task of creating a new political order to the civilian bureaucracy, nascent political parties, and civil society groups.

Tunisia's new government faces major challenges to dismantle Ben Ali's security regime and to ensure the transition to democratic rule with civilian oversight over the instruments of force.

The abuses of Tunisia's internal security institutions and the impunity with which they acted against ordinary citizens served as a catalyst for the protests that ended Ben Ali's rule. Reforming or otherwise dismantling this large and complex sector will be no easy task. But it is an essential component of constructing a new social contract in Tunisia.

Why Security Sector Reform?

Security sector reform (SSR) is a comprehensive tool for fixing the dysfunctional security sectors in fragile states that are emerging from conflict, developing capacities to meet the human security needs of their populations, or transitioning from authoritarian rule.[5] SSR is also an important tool for the prevention of conflict. In many fragile states, the security institutions are themselves a major source of insecurity. Transforming the security sector into one that is democratically accountable and functions in accordance with the rule of law is an important step toward averting the recurrence of insecurity and conflict and preventing newly democratic or transitioning regimes from reverting to authoritarian rule.

The SSR agenda is an ambitious one. SSR aims to address a range of security-related challenges. These include: 1) the lack of statutory security providers due to inadequate institutions, poor training, or corruption; 2) the presence of armed nonstate actors, gangs, and other nonstatutory security providers; 3) the absence of legitimate and effective formal or informal justice institutions; and 4) the lack of effective, transparent governance of the security sector. Yet, how these challenges present themselves in a particular fragile state will vary according to legacies of conflict; tribal, ethnic, or religious patterns; systems of government; colonial legacies; the level of economic development; environmental conditions; the vibrancy of civil society; and transnational influences, to name but a few. In other words, there is no formula for SSR that will be applicable to all states.

Tunisia is well positioned to undertake SSR. With a small territory and relatively homogeneous population, Tunisia features a large and educated middle class, a liberalized economy, a youth bulge that is diminishing, and a history of encouraging socioeconomic freedoms, particularly for women.[6] For example, Tunisian election law mandates that party lists be comprised equally of both male and female candidates. Twenty-seven percent of the members of the National Constituent Assembly are women. Women serve in the military and constitute more than 50 percent of university students. Additionally, despite the significant constraints on speech and protest, Tunisia under Ben Ali featured both legal and illegal opposition parties, and a range of civil society groups that engaged in muted opposition to the government.

Tunisia has a vibrant legal community, a bar association, a lawyers union, and civil society groups, many of which were active even under Ben Ali. Civil society activists under Ben Ali were able to monitor the government's activities through the publication of laws and amendments, as well as appointments. Tunisia also has a well-developed legal code that, in principle, proscribes the functions of the government. There are 1,700 laws and amendments that govern the security sector alone (there is no legislation governing the intelligence sector). Although the extent to which these laws are still in effect is as yet unclear, they do provide a foundation on which to reform the security sector and its oversight mechanisms.

Tunisia also has significant security capacity. Although the country is small in size relative to other Middle East and North Africa (MENA) states, its armed forces have ably filled the vacuum created by the collapse of Ben Ali's security apparatus and the defections of police throughout the country. While providing internal security, the armed forces have also secured the maritime and land borders, countered cross-border incursions from Libyan armed groups, and established five refugee camps for 1.6 million refugees, mostly from sub-Saharan Africa, fleeing the violence in Libya.[7] The armed forces clearly ascribe to the concept of civilian oversight of the military, and although they are currently fulfilling a number of internal security tasks, they have publicly, and repeatedly, stated their intention to return to the barracks when the police can again fulfill their security functions.

One of the most striking features in Tunisian society, even a year after the revolution, is the veritable explosion of public discourse and debate. As one senior military officer noted, Tunisians "never used to talk about politics. Now we talk about politics all the time. We have so much freedom now. We almost don't know what to do with it."[8] Every evening, Tunisia's three television stations devote their evening programming to debates on every subject imaginable. Recently, for example, a long debate between the President of the Tunisian League for Human Rights and a salafist student addressed the right to wear the *niqab* (the Muslim face veil for women) at school. "Tunisia has become a debating society," Radwan Masmoudi, Director of the Center for the Study of Islam and Democracy, observed.[9]

Another metric of change is the number of political parties. Under Ben Ali there were five official political parties. During the October 2011 election, there were 111. A civil society activist told us that "all Tunisians are learning what democracy is and how it really works. We don't really have political parties, and the parties we have don't really know yet how to act like parties or what role they should play in the opposition."[10] Yet, these parties competed for seats in the National Constituent Assembly in Tunisia's first postrevolutionary elections, which were widely heralded to be free and fair.

Civil society has also burgeoned. Some 2,000 new civil society groups have emerged in Tunisia since the revolution. Although many of these groups are still virtual, they are pushing for a voice in the Tunisian transition—demanding transparency, and fueling the Tunisian "debating society," particularly among Tunisian youth. According to Omar Mestiri, director of Radio Kalima, "post-revolutionary media is now delivering journalist materials more representative of Tunisian society. Now, there is more space for different opinions and dialogue."[11] In the year since the fall of Ben Ali's regime, Tunisia gained four new cable channels, 12 radio stations, and 18 newspapers.[12]

Although the prospects for SSR in Tunisia are perhaps better than in any other MENA state following the Arab Spring, substantial challenges remain.[13] The *raison d'être* of Ben Ali's security institutions was to protect the regime, not the population. The transition to democratic rule will require a fundamental reorientation of the mandate and institutional culture of the labyrinth of security institutions that constitute the Tunisian security sector. SSR will be critical for building trust in the government and its security institutions and central to the construct of a national narrative that undergirds a new social contract between the people of Tunisia and its government.

Mapping Tunisia's Security Sector

What are the prospects for SSR in Tunisia? What progress has been made in the year since the fall of the Ben Ali regime? What gaps remain, and how best can these gaps be addressed? To answer these questions, we will map the security sector in Tunisia, assess the status of reform efforts currently underway, if any, and identify gaps. Four categories of actors, institutions, and functions comprise Tunisia's security sector: (1) statutory security providers; (2) governance and democratic oversight; (3) justice and the rule of law; and (4) civil society. We will conclude by proposing additional steps that the Tunisian government and the international community can undertake to address those gaps, realize Tunisia's security sector transformation, and support the country's transition to democratic rule.

Statutory Security Providers

Statutory security providers typically include all state institutions with a formal mandate to ensure the safety of the state and its citizens, such as the armed forces, police, gendarmerie, intelligence services, and border and customs guards. In Tunisia, the statutory security providers are part of the Ministry of National Defense (MOD) and the Ministry of Interior and Local Development (MOI). There are also forces assigned to the Ministry of Justice (MOJ). The intelligence capabilities are assigned to the Ministries of Defense, Interior, and Foreign Affairs.

The Armed Forces. The Tunisian Armed Forces (*Forces Armees Tunisiens*) are small, well disciplined, and widely respected for their refusal to follow orders to use lethal force against their countrymen. Their inaction makes them stand out compared to the armed forces of other MENA nations. They are unique in the region for other reasons as well. The Tunisian military, unlike the armed forces of other MENA countries, is completely subordinate to the government and controlled by it. Consequently, the Tunisian armed forces never played a political role, nor did they legitimize the former regime.[14] Additionally, Tunisia's armed forces are not economically invested in the old regime. Unlike the Egyptian military, Tunisia's armed forces did not receive any special compensation or material advantages for their service to the state.[15]

In discussions with senior members of the armed forces, they openly admit that in Ben Ali's hierarchy of security institutions, they were at the bottom. "We were always last," noted one senior officer. "The regime did not like us," another noted. Indeed, in my conversations with military officers, it became clear that the military's distance from the regime was deliberately created by President Bourguiba, Tunisia's founding president, who feared a possible coup and sought to institutionalize the military's distance from the center of power.[16] Ben Ali, who was himself a former Interior Minister, continued this policy, while buttressing the capabilities and size of the MOI security forces.

Both Bourguiba and Ben Ali kept the armed forces deliberately out of the center of power. Conscript-filled military ranks were deployed to less-populated regions of the country to do public works projects. Deployments were chiefly for peacekeeping missions in Africa, which kept the armed forces engaged elsewhere. A generation of officers was educated in the war colleges and command and staff colleges in the United States through International Military Education and Training (IMET) and the Counterterrorism Fellowship Program (CTFP). The military was kept small, numbering between 40,000 and 43,000 forces.

The Tunisian Armed Forces include the Army, Navy, and the Air Force. The Army numbers only 27,000 soldiers, and the Navy has no deep-water ships. The Air Force has less than 20 working helicopters and only 20 combat capable aircraft.[17] Yet, the Army's participation in United Nations (UN) peacekeeping missions gave it the essential experience to fill the void left by the security forces as Ben Ali's government collapsed. The armed forces quickly moved to protect key infrastructure, restore law and order, and maintain security and stability. A year after the revolution, 18,000 soldiers continue to guard some 700 buildings and vital installations. In addition to assuming traditional internal security functions, the armed forces also face serious challenges along Tunisia's land and maritime borders. Some 1.6 million refugees from Libya's civil war, mostly from sub-Saharan Africa, crossed into Tunisia, and some 30,000 Tunisians fled to Lampedusa, an island off the coast of Italy.[18]

The stark contrast between the impunity of the internal security services and the measured restraint of the armed forces is reflected in how the two organizations are publicly viewed. Whereas the security forces are reviled and hated, the armed forces are viewed as belonging to the people. "The Army is one of us!" has been a rallying cry at demonstrations.

Compared to those of other MENA nations, the Tunisian Armed Forces were also funded at much lower levels in both absolute and relative terms as a percentage of gross domestic product (GDP). For example, in 2009, Tunisian military expenditures were 1.2 percent of GDP, whereas Libya and Egypt's military spending was 2.8 percent and 3.3 percent, respectively.[19] Ministry officials noted that both Bourguiba and Ben Ali had kept the military's capabilities small, but "sufficient for our mission."

A year after the revolution, this assessment remains unchanged. Ministry officials rank the priorities of the Tunisian government to be economic, with national security—particularly the control of borders—as subordinate. When asked whether the Tunisian military has sufficient equipment to accomplish its expanded mission since the revolution, the response was a surprising affirmative. "We have the manpower we need. We managed to go through the revolution and do all that we do with what we have. . . . We do not need expensive weapons or aircraft—perhaps only helicopters."[20]

In a formal ministry briefing, senior military officers noted that "the reform of the defense and the security sector requires a political system based on good governance." In addition to a commitment to transparency, officials noted that the Army must be open to different political and social actors, and that its budgets must be available for public scrutiny. "The term 'classified' or 'top secret' must not constitute, under any condition, an obstacle to the transparency of the defense budget." They also embraced the concept of democratic oversight, noting that it is "imperative" that there be parliamentary oversight of reforms of the Ministry and of the progress of those reforms.[21]

In minimizing and sidelining the military, Ben Ali created a professional, apolitical institution that was little known—and little feared. Before General Ammar emerged a national hero, he was an unknown. Yet, his actions propelled the Tunisian Armed Forces to a position of preeminence—the institution that protected the Tunisian state and the Tunisian people, not the corrupt regime. Having expressed a preference for the barracks over politics, the armed forces emerged as one of the only respected institutions of the previous regime.

The unique attributes of the Tunisian Armed Forces—its credibility, commitment to assuming its traditional functions, and its skill and willingness to assume an internal peacekeeping mission—suggest that the scope for reform of the military is very small. There will be challenges adjusting to a democratic system of governance and parliamentary oversight. Yet, the need for oversight is recognized and welcomed by the senior officers we spoke to as being essential to democratic governance. Another task will be a strategic one—military officers are keen to engage in the drafting of national strategies now that the exercise is no longer top down by fiat. Indeed, senior military officers seek to expand their role as subject matter experts and to support civilian decisionmakers in the ministry, as their counterparts do in most democratic nations. The armed forces appear well poised to tackle these tasks.

One senior military officer observed that the reform of any one ministry is closely tied to the reform of other ministries, and that the reform of the Ministry of Interior will be critical for determining how quickly the armed forces can cease conducting internal security functions. But until the legitimacy and capacity of the MOI is addressed and improved, the armed forces will likely continue to provide an internal security function, although increasingly in a supporting role.

The Internal Security Forces. As much as the armed forces are admired as the heroes of the revolution, the police are widely reviled for keeping Ben Ali and his family in power, for imprisioning and torturing Tunisians who ran afoul of that regime, and for shooting civilians during the protests. During a recent visit, I was told that the unpopularity of particular ministries can be measured by the amount of barbed wire around their buildings. A year after the fall of Ben Ali, the MOI was still surrounded by concertina wire a few layers deep—more to protect those inside than to barricade the ministry. Army tanks also stood guard. The impression was of a ministry under siege.

The internal security forces controlled by the MOI include the police, the National Guard, the Judicial Police (which operates in the Ministry of Justice and the courts, but is controlled by the Ministry of Interior), the Intervention Forces (Special Weapons and Tactics [SWAT] forces), and the Presidential Guard Forces. The internal security forces are almost byzantine in their complexity, and the organizational chart of the MOI remains classified, which complicates the task of mapping the internal security structures controlled by the MOI, as well as the oversight mechanisms within the Ministry.

It is also difficult to establish the size of the security forces. There are no officially published statistics, and the ministry website offers no details—it is the only ministry on the Tunisian government website with an empty tab. Media reports have estimated the security forces to number from 150,000 to 200,000, although subsequent ministry announcements acknowledged that those numbers were deliberately inflated. Actual internal security forces are estimated to number between 40,000 and 80,000, approximately half of which are part-time augmentation forces or paid informants. The higher figure accords with the ministry payroll.[22] According to Mohammad Lazhar Akremi, the Minister Delegate to the Minister of Interior in Charge of Reforms under the previous transitional government, internal security forces (police, National Guard, and civil defense forces) numbered 49,000 before the overthrow of the Ben Ali regime. The police subsequently recruited an additional 12,000 forces, bringing the total to 61,000.[23] New recruits were needed to inject new untainted officers into the force, to manage the rise in crime, weapons, and drug trafficking, and to replace the forces that had disappeared after the fall of the regime. However, the training program for these new recruits has not been reformed.

The police include both the regular police and the political police, which were reportedly disbanded during the transitional government of Beji Caid Essebsi in March 2011. The political police were fully integrated with the regular police, but operated under a parallel hierarchy. The political police maintain the secret files; two copies of each are currently kept at the Ministry of Interior, where ministry officials claim they are safe. However, individuals who have left the police or the MOI have reported that files have been burned. Tunisian law currently prohibits publication of these files for 50 years. Although not as extensive as the files of some other totalitarian regimes, they contain a great deal of potentially damaging and possibly false information. Who actually controls the files is unclear.[24] The release on January 18, 2012, of a video on YouTube and Facebook depicting the newly appointed Minister of Interior, Ali Laarayedh, reportedly engaged in a sexual act in a prison cell suggests that it is not the Minister of Interior who controls the files.[25]

Whereas the police operate mostly in urban areas, the National Guard operates in the coastal and rural areas where the revolution began. Described as a paramilitary organization or a gendarmerie, the National Guard numbers approximately 12,000. National Guard forces man checkpoints, and there is a small fleet of patrol boats for customs and border protection operations. The Guard reportedly also has a counterterrorism capability consisting of the National Guard Commando Group, the National Guard Special Unit, and the Tunisian Anti-Terrorism Brigade.[26]

The Judicial Police are part of the Ministry of Interior but work within the Judiciary. They are the investigative arm of the internal security forces with responsibility for collecting evidence, conducting investigations, and writing the formal reports of the investigations for cases before the courts. The Judicial Police do not have the tools to do professional investigations. According to Judiciary lawyers, the Judicial Police do not have the capacity for fingerprinting, DNA testing, or other means of collecting evidence. Their investigations rely solely on confession. The confession becomes the basis for the investigation report, which is the sole means by which evidence is submitted in the court before the judge. Under the Ben Ali regime, the Judicial Police used violence and torture during their interrogations, both to extract confessions and to force the accused to sign the confessions. There is no provision for the presence of legal counsel from the moment of arrest to the conclusion of the investigation.[27]

The Presidential Guard Forces (PGF) are also part of the Ministry of Interior. There are no reliable estimates or officially published records to determine the size of the PGF. Their principle duty was to protect the President and his family. During the demonstrations in January 2011, the Presidential Guard reportedly fired on demonstrators and battled the Tunisian armed forces.[28] The testimony of Ali Seriati, the former Presidential Security Chief, during the trial for his role in the deaths of protesters, revealed that the PGF had not only snipers but also water cannons and other crowd-suppression capabilities.[29] This suggests that the PFG's mandate under Ben Ali was quite broad.

A strong current in Tunisian society seeks justice, if not revenge. Many police fled as the government collapsed, and others have remained in their homes or elsewhere with family, fearing that there will be retribution for their roles both before and during the revolution. Some 250-300 police stations were burned, and in several towns in the interior of Tunisia, the attacks took a more personal turn with the burning of policemen's homes.

The police are fearful that they will be targeted for revenge or prosecuted for their roles in Ben Ali's security apparatus. This fear has limited their ability to perform normal police functions. The sudden reversal from a position of power and respect to one of weakness and derision has generated frustration, fear, and anger. Police syndicates have organized strikes to draw attention to their plight and to call for improved working conditions and government protection while on duty.[30] These strikes have sparked large counterdemonstrations with protestors shouting, "Go Back to Work," and carrying placards with slogans like "People Want to Purge the Ministry of Interior."[31] Adel Jebali, a member of the National Union for Security Forces, one of the police syndicates, noted that "people perceive us to be criminals."[32]

Tunisia has a great deal of police capacity. Senior officers are often highly educated, and many have attended police training academies in Europe. Educational standards are also quite high for entrance into the police force. Police currently are educated alongside military officers at the military academy, although there is a proposal to create a separate police academy. There is also a solid police infrastructure (e.g., police stations, communications equipment, vehicles, and uniforms). Training is standardized, and even Rules of Engagement have been established. The problem is that all of these remain largely unchanged from the Ben Ali regime. Under Ben Ali, the police were responsible for serious human rights violations, including illegal and arbitrary arrests, torture, and extrajudicial executions. According to a National Guard officer, "The competence was there, but the climate was terrible."[33]

The current Minister of Interior, Ali Laarayedh, was himself tortured during the 16 years he was jailed by the Ben Ali regime. He is an interesting choice for the Interior Ministry—one that the previously banned Ennahda Party was at first hesitant to fill. After Ennahda won a plurality in the national elections and began selecting cabinet members, some of the party leadership were concerned that the appointment of an interior minister from Ennahda would generate the perception that the party was intent on revenge. The party leadership was wary of a potential misstep that could fuel further fear, particularly within the ministry and among its personnel. But in the run-up to the October elections, two senior members of Ennahda, both of whom had been imprisoned and tortured under Ben Ali, were invited to a meeting with interior ministry officials and the leaders of the two police syndicates. The meeting had been arranged by the syndicates, and the request was made that Ennahda fill the position of the new Minister of Interior after the elections.

This first meeting was followed by others, and the two senior leaders began to engage regularly with the syndicates. In a conversation over Ennahda's intentions, the two Ennahda leaders reassured the attendees, telling them that despite being among the worst tortured members of the Ennahda party, "We do not hold it against you. We need reform," they told their audience. "We need to turn the page and look to the future." One of the Ennahda leaders recognized the man who had tortured him in the audience. This man asked his former victim, "Do you hate us?" The Ennahda leader said, "No. You were a screw within the engine. If it wasn't you, it would have been someone else."

In relating this story, the Ennahda leader emphasized that the party would "never allow anyone to pursue revenge." Moved to tears, he added, "I do not want compensation for my suffering. . . . The only thing that will save me is to see my country the way I want. It would be a gross mistake if we fail to deliver an inclusive system for everyone."[34]

There are positive indications that reform of the interior ministry has been a priority for Tunisia's transitional governments. In May 2011, the MOI reached out to the Geneva Center for the Democratic Control of the Armed Forces (DCAF) to undertake a preliminary study of the Ministry's communication with the public. The Communication Review, released in September 2011, offers a series of recommendations intended to "restore confidence between citizens and security forces."[35] In November, 2011, *Le Labo' Démocratique*, a civil society group, together with DCAF, organized an international conferences on the archives of the secret police to help the MOI explore how best to manage the archives and how to establish parliamentary control over MOI intelligence capabilities.[36]

The most comprehensive plan for reform of Tunisia's security sector is the Ministry of Interior white paper, entitled "Security and Development: A White Paper for Democratic Security in Tunisia."[37] The report was released by Tunisia's interim President, Foued Mebazaa, and Akremi. Akremi was nominated to the ministry in July 2011 to lead the reform effort and was charged by the Minister of the Interior, Habib El Essid, to draft a white paper with proposals for reform that would be specifically targeted to the needs of Tunisia. Akremi called upon experts throughout the ministry and from France, Spain, and Switzerland to participate in drafting the proposal, and the draft white paper was submitted for review to a seminar in September 2011.[38] The final document contains their critiques.[39]

According to the white paper, the proposed reform of the Tunisian security sector "can be summarized as moving from a police order to a police service that can respond urgently to the new challenges of crime." To achieve this objective, "all the levers of modernization should be mobilized at the same time: reconciliation of the National Police and the National Guard, redistribution of responsibilities between municipalities and the state security services, and implementation of local security, modernization of human resource management, optimization and sharing of material, and finally, citizen control."[40]

The report recognizes and addresses many of the key issues for reform of the MOI. The opacity of the ministry with regard to its labyrinth security structures and actors is addressed through a reorganization of the security services into three bodies—the National Guard, the National Police, and Civil Protection—and the merger of civilian and uniformed National Police.[41] Recruitment and training are treated extensively in a separate chapter, which recommends the creation of a Tunisian police academy, new salary hierarchies and career management mechanisms, and an overall emphasis on professionalism and ethics in recruitment, training, and advancement. Another chapter is devoted to the public image of the security services.

The report notes that no communication plan alone can change a "bad image." The MOI's image will only transform "when the professional practices of all its agents are transformed."[42] Mechanisms to accomplish this transformation include not only new uniforms and open reception areas in police stations and guard bureaus, but also new codes of conduct and greater police transparency.[43] Notable are the calls for reforms of policy custody practices, police intelligence, and techniques for video surveillance and electronic monitoring, and the banning of imprisonment for religious or political ideas.

Currently, the white paper constitutes the only sector-wide roadmap for reforming Tunisia's security sector. It clearly acknowledges and addresses the critical challenges in transforming the institution and culture of the MOI. Although the report was prepared by the previous transitional government as an MOI input for the work of the Constituent Assembly, it appears unlikely that the new government will adopt its assessment and recommendations. When asked about the utility of the white paper as a roadmap for reform, members of the Ennahda political bureau acknowledged that although the report contains useful suggestions, it is a product of the "old regime." Ennahda seeks to draw upon the expertise of a wide and inclusive group of experts, including not only Italian and French, but also British, American, Swiss, and South African, to develop a new SSR plan. Ennahda emphasized the importance of the inclusion of Tunisian experts because the model developed must ultimately meet "their aspirations."[44]

Intelligence Agencies. The Intelligence Agency is part of the Ministry of Interior, although there are also intelligence functions in the Ministry of Defense and the Ministry of Foreign Affairs. Information on the intelligence community is not widely available. The white paper, however, devotes a final chapter to intelligence reform. The report cautions that failure to reform the intelligence function will leave "a small minority of decision makers" with a monopoly of "the power of knowledge."[45] To guard against this situation, the paper recommends creating a National Intelligence Agency with clearly defined objectives and a legal framework under which to operate. The proposed agency would also be subject to strict controls at two levels—ministry control and parliamentary control.[46] Personnel would include both military and civilians. Domestic intelligence collection would be prohibited.[47] The Intelligence Agency would be removed from the MOI and report directly to the president of the republic.[48]

The Intelligence Agency would also have a coordinating function. The white paper proposes that the agency coordinate collection and analysis for a National Intelligence Council. This council would be chaired by a head of state or head of government as determined by the future constitution and would include two members of the National Assembly.[49] The white paper also recommends creating a parliamentary committee in the National Assembly that would include a few members with special clearances who would exercise oversight of the agency's activities and its budget. Two parliamentary committee members would also serve on the National Intelligence Council.[50]

There are currently no laws governing the intelligence sector.[51] A sound legal framework is a precondition for effective, efficient, and accountable security governance, particularly over the intelligence sector. Tunisia will need a legal framework that defines the roles and missions, the intelligence institutions and functions, and the prerogatives and limits of the intelligence organizations and their members.[52] Equally important will be undertaking reforms with enough transparency to build public trust and confidence in a function intimately tied to the abuses of the previous regime.

Governance and Democratic Oversight

The second key piece of Tunisia's security sector is governance and democratic oversight. These are found in the executive functions of Tunisia's transition governments, the Ministries of Defense and Interior, the three national commissions, and the National Constituent Assembly—the democratically elected parliamentary body with a mandate to draft a new constitution for the Republic of Tunisia.

The First Transition Government, January 17-February 27, 2011. The first transition government was created in the immediate aftermath of Ben Ali's departure. On January 17, 2011, Prime Minister Mohammad Ghannouchi named a new interim unity government. The 19 ministers included six members of Ben Ali's cabinet—including the three critical Defense, Interior and Foreign Affairs Ministries—three opposition leaders, and 10 independents. The interim government sought to begin crafting a new narrative contrasting it with its predecessors. In addition to including opposition members in the government, promises were made to free political prisoners and to include international monitors at the upcoming elections; furthermore, political groups, including Islamist parties, were granted amnesty. The transition government also created three national commissions, which began work on January 19, 2011. (These will be discussed in further detail below). However, the participation of Ben Ali loyalists sparked a new round of violent protests. Five ministers defected from the interim government soon after it was formed, and Ghannouchi replaced the Ministers of Interior, Defense, and Foreign Affairs. Finally, as protests continued to mount, Ghannouchi himself resigned on February 27, 2011, and Beji Caid Essebsi, a former foreign minister under Bourguiba, became the new Prime Minister.[53]

The Second Transition Government, February 27- December 24, 2011. The second transition government under Beji Caid Essebsi sought to address protestors' demands, particularly the charge that the dismantling of Ben Ali's security establishment was not moving apace. He appointed a new cabinet largely comprised of technocrats who had not served under Ben Ali's government. The new government announced the dissolution of Ben Ali's political police and his ruling party, the *Rassemblement Constitutionnel Démocratique* (RCD), in March 2011.[54] Despite progress, antigovernment protests and violent street battles in Tunis reflected a deep-seated dissatisfaction with the pace of change and fear that the new government would revert to autocratic rule.

Yet, in the midst of ongoing protests, the second interim government made two critical decisions: first, to place constitutional reform ahead of elections; and second, to delay the elections for a National Constituent Assembly from July to October 2011. The first decision ensured that the old constitution, which privileged the RCD and thus made free and fair elections virtually impossible, would not return the old ruling party or Ben Ali's political establishment to power. The second delayed the transitional period, so that reformist and opposition parties would be afforded the opportunity to compete and to shape the drafting of a new constitution for Tunisia.[55]

More than 90 percent of registered Tunisian citizens participated in what was Tunisia's first truly competitive election since it declared independence from France in 1956.[56] The previously banned Islamist Ennahda Party won a plurality of 89 of the 217 seats in the National Constituent Assembly.[57]

The Caretaker Government, December 23, 2011-present. The Ennahda Party combined with the secular Congress for the Republic Party and the left Ettakatol Party to form a caretaker government to run the country during the year-long period in which the Assembly is charged with drafting a new constitution.[58] Hamadi Jebali, Ennahda's secretary general, is the new Prime Minister, and Moncef Marzouki, head of the Congress for the Republic, holds the largely ceremonial post of Tunisian President. At its first meeting, the Assembly confirmed the selection of Mustafa Ben Jaafar, leader of the Ettakatol party, as speaker of the new assembly.

The new Prime Minister, Hamadi Jebali, proposed a cabinet, which was approved on December 23, 2011. Only the Minister of Defense, Abdelkarim Zbidi, remained unchanged from the previous cabinet.

The Constituent Assembly approved Tunisia's new government but did not stipulate when the government's mandate would end. Given the 1-year mandate for the drafting of the constitution, the assumption was that elections would shortly follow completion of the constitution in late 2012 or early 2013. But in February 2012, Prime Minister Jebali announced that elections would not be held until August 2013.[59] One month later, Jebali announced that elections would be held no later than June 2013, and preferably on April 9, Tunisia Martyr's Day.[60] The delays may simply reflect the government's recognition that drafting a new constitution in only a year is not feasible (in South Africa, the new constitution was drafted in 2 years). However, civil society groups and opposition parties have expressed concern over the government's open mandate. Former Prime Minister Beji Caid Essebsi has called for the National Constituent Assembly to respect the mandate to draft the constitution and prepare for elections within a period not exceeding October 23, 2012.

The Ministry of Defense. Civilian oversight and governance of the Tunisian Armed Forces are assigned to the Tunisian MOD, led by a civilian Minister of Defense. The MOD is an almost entirely civilian organization. It has primary responsibility for the implementation of policy decisions regarding the uniformed services. The Chief of Staff of the Armed Forces is the principle advisor to the Minister. The Chiefs of Staff of each of the three services—Army, Air Force, and Navy—command each of their respective services but do not serve on a unified general staff. Coordination among the services is the responsibility of the Chief of Staff of the Armed Forces.

The Ministry of Defense is comprised of the Ministerial Cabinet, the Chief of Staff of the Armed Forces, and the National Defense Institute, the senior military defense university. The MOD oversees seven directorates for military justice, general conscription and mobilization, central administration, personnel and training, information and culture, military health, and the "National Military Mutuality," as well as the High Committee of the Armed Forces, "specialized instruments," technical departments, and military schools.[61]

The Minister of Defense's specific authorities are defined by a 1975 Presidential Decree, which specifies that the Minister of Defense serves the President of the Republic, who is the Supreme Commander of the Armed Forces. The Minister of Defense has the task of ensuring the security and integrity of national territory and the protection of people's lives.

As in the case of the armed forces, the scope of reform of the MOD is quite small. The Ministry will need to adjust to a democratic system of governance that will likely involve regular review and oversight by parliamentary committees of the MOD and its budget. This will require institutionalizing a culture of oversight and adjusting processes and procedures to accommodate external review. Yet, the need for oversight is recognized and welcomed by the Ministry, suggesting that the MOD will not resist these changes. Another likely reform will involve the inclusion of both civilians and military officers in the drafting of national strategies and strategic planning, a role that military officers did not fulfill in the Ben Ali regime. Senior military officers are keen to fill the role of subject matter experts and to support civilian decisionmakers, as their counterparts do in most democratic nations.

The Ministry of Interior. The Ministry of Interior is the proverbial black box of Tunisia's security sector. Successful SSR in Tunisia will ultimately hinge on the establishment of real, democratically elected, civilian oversight of the MOI. Tunisian human rights activists characterize the current relationship between Minister of Interior Laarayedh and his Ministry as "a war."[62]

The standoff between the Minister of Interior and the director of one of the ministry's subordinate security forces in January 2012 dramatically underscores this point. Laarayedh sought to remove Monsef Al Ajimi, the Director of the Intervention Forces, from his post. Ajimi had been formally accused of firing on crowds in Thala during the revolution. But Ajimi had the loyalty of some 12,000 police from the Bouchoucha Barracks, who physically blocked access to the accused director and then organized a strike in protest of his attempted removal. Across Tunis, key installations were left with no Tunisian security presence, including the embassies. One of the police unions intervened, persuading the strikers that their interests were not being served by supporting a senior member of the Ben Ali security apparatus—a man who had fired on the people. The courts have not yet ruled on the case, and although the strikes ceased, the Minister of Interior was forced to move the accused director to a consultant position elsewhere in the ministry.

Both the video release and the thwarted attempt to fire the Director of the Intervention Forces suggest that Laarayedh's authority over the ministry—and thus, the authority of the civilian transition government approved by the nationally elected Constituent Assembly—is quite limited. It also suggests that ministry officials are likely to resist efforts to reform the Ministry, and, as the incident of the Intervention Forces suggests, that they have the capacity and the resources to do so. According to a legal activist engaged in promoting security sector reform, "Senior officers in the MOI do not have the intention to do reform. Those senior officers are not collaborating with the new government. They are resisting any reform and are seeking to protect their interests, their positions, and themselves."[63]

Three National Commissions. The three commissions created within days of Ben Ali's overthrow constitute another important element through which civilian authority over Tunisia's transition to democratic rule is exercised. The three commissions are the National Commission to Investigate Violence During the Riots, headed by Tawfik Bouderbala; the National Commission to Investigate Corruption, headed by Abdelfattah Amor; and the High Commission for the Fulfillment of Revolutionary Goals, Political Reform, and Democratic Transition, headed by Iyadh Ben Achour.

The most important of these three commissions is the High Commission for the Fulfillment of Revolutionary Goals, Political Reform, and Democratic Transition, headed by Ben Achour. Also known as the Ben Achour Commission, it includes 154 technical experts, legal advisors, and members of Tunisia's political parties and civil society. According to Albert Stepan, "This Commission is one of the most successful and consensual organizations in the history of crafting a democratic transition."[64]

The Ben Achour Commission began work on January 19, only days after the fall of the Ben Ali regime. On April 11, 2011, members of the Commission approved a number of documents that defined the post-Ben Ali transition to democratic rule, each of which was subsequently implemented. First was the decision to create a Constituent Assembly to produce a new constitution and to hold Tunisia's first elections for seats in this assembly. Second, the Commission agreed that the Constituent Assembly would appoint a government and that this government would be responsible to the Constituent Assembly. Third, the Commission adopted a proportional representation electoral system and required that party lists contain alternating male and female candidates. Fourth, the commission invited international observers to monitor the elections and created an independent electoral commission by moving the *Instance Supérieure Indépendante pour les Élections* (ISIE) out of the Ministry of Interior. Finally, the Commission agreed to dissolve the RCD and ban some of its leaders from participation in the elections for the Constituent Assembly. Other party members, however, were permitted to form new parties and to participate in the election.[65]

The commission appointed two other national commissions to respond to civil society demands for transparency and justice. The National Commission to Investigate Violence During the Riots was headed by Tawfik Bouderbala, the former president of the Tunisian Human Rights League. The Commission was quickly overwhelmed with claims, even though the Commission is limited only to the 2-to-3-month time frame of the demonstrations immediately before and during the revolution. The second commission, the National Commission to Investigate Corruption, was headed by Abdel Fattah, a Special Rapporteur for the former UN Human Rights Committee and a political science professor.[66] All three commissions are currently at a standstill. The chair of the corruption committee died from an apparent heart attack, and the other two commissions are awaiting guidance from the Constituent Assembly and the transitional government. The National Commission to Investigate Violence During the Riots will reportedly release its findings in late-spring 2012.[67]

The National Constituent Assembly. During the transitional period, the 217-seat National Constituent Assembly is Tunisia's legislative body. It has a clear mandate to draft a new constitution for Tunisia during 2012. What is less clear is the interim government's mandate for reform. Although the Constituent Assembly approved the caretaker government headed by Prime Minister Hemadi Jebali, this does not necessarily confer a mandate to reform the government or the security sector before the Constituent Assembly has drafted a new constitution and before elections for a new government are held at a yet-to-be-determined date in 2013.

The Constituent Assembly has made some progress. Its members adopted a "mini-constitution" in December 2011 that defines government and parliamentary authority until the new constitution is complete. In mid-January, members also approved internal bylaws to govern the constitution-drafting process.[68] Article 111 creates a commission to draft the constitution, and, on January 18, 2012, Ben Jaafar was appointed head of this commission. It coordinates the work of six other committees that will focus on: 1) introduction, basic principles, and constitutional review; 2) rights and freedoms; 3) legislative and executive powers, and relations between powers; 4) civil, administrative, financial and constitutional justice; 5) constitutional bodies, including all committees, focused on media pluralism, financial regulation, separation of politics and religion, and law enforcement and security; and 6) local, regional and municipal issues.[69] Particularly encouraging was the adoption of transparency rules during the constitution-drafting process. According to Article 62, "Public information is the rule, secrecy is the exception. It is up for the members of the committee to decide [when exceptions will be made]."[70]

Justice and the Rule of Law

The third component of the Tunisian security sector consists of the justice functions as they relate to the security sector and the rule of law. This includes the Ministry of Justice and its prison regimes, the judiciary, and prosecution services.

The Ministry of Justice overseas the application of Tunisian law, including the offices of the regional and national judiciary and the administration of prisons and rehabilitation centers.[71] According to a 1974 Presidential Decree, the Ministry of Justice is responsible for developing and implementing judicial policy; drafting legislation and commenting on draft legislation submitted by other ministries; drafting international conventions; organizing and inspecting judicial public services; and considering applications for pardon, parole, rehabilitation, and revision.[72] Subsequently, with the inclusion of ministry oversight of the prison system and human rights, the ministry's functions also included the execution of sentences and the promotion of human rights.[73]

The General Directorate of Prisons and Rehabilitation (GDSR), which oversees the Tunisian prison system, is one of the subordinate organizations of the Ministry of Justice.[74] Interestingly, it is currently being run by an Army Senior Colonel (one-star equivalent).[75]

There are 35 confinement facilities under the GDSR, including one prison housing strictly women and seven juvenile detention and rehabilitation centers.[76] In February 2011, a general amnesty law authorized the release of 500 political prisoners.

The Tunisian Judiciary has three levels of regular courts—Cantonal, First Instance, and Appeals. At the apex is the Court of Cassation. At each level, the courts have sections for civil, commercial, criminal, social, and personal status cases (there are no specialized Sharia courts). The High Court, according to Article 68, meets for cases of high treason committed by a member of the government.[77]

According to Article 65 of the Tunisian Constitution, "The judiciary is independent; the magistrates in the exercise of their functions are not subjected to any authority other than the law."[78] In practice, however, the executive has almost exclusive control over the judiciary. The Tunisian president chairs the Superior Council of Magistrates (*Le Conseil supérieur de la magistrature*), which recommends judges (magistrates); the Tunisian president also appoints judges. The Minister of Justice also serves on the Superior Council, and the Ministry administers the judiciary and its budget and determines the number of judges needed and their assignments. Reportedly under Ben Ali, the Ministry even determined case assignments and intervened to ensure favorable rulings for members of the Ben Ali establishment.[79] The Minister of Justice can also transfer judges and prosecutors without their consent for punitive reasons or to intimidate. A recent European Union Justice Peer Review Report on Tunisia, published in December 2011, recommends "immediate steps" to restore public confidence in the justice system and the establishment of an independent and effective justice system founded on the principles of judicial independence and the impartiality and irrevocability of judges and prosecutors.[80]

The prosecution system in Tunisia is largely judicial, and prosecutors are comparable to judges. Trials are by judge, not jury. Prosecutors are part of the Ministry of Justice, although the Judicial Police, who conduct investigations and prepare the report for prosecution, are part of the Ministry of Interior. The Youth Lawyers Association and the Lawyers Union have proposed reforms of both the prosecutorial system and the role of the Judicial Police. One recommendation is to allow legal counsel to be present during interrogations conducted by the Judicial Police. In January 2012, association representatives met with the minister of justice, who reportedly told them that it was not possible to move away from an interrogation-based system. Reforming the prosecutorial system and the Judicial Police, as these groups proposed, would require training the police to conduct real investigations, transferring the

Judicial Police to the MOJ and training lawyers to advocate for their clients during interrogation. The representatives concluded that the enormous institutional obstacles and time constraints limit the will to undertake serious political reform.[81]

The Lawyers Union and the Youth Lawyers Association are able to submit their proposed reforms to the Constituent Assembly, particularly on issues relating to judiciary reform and human rights laws. However, they noted that the Assembly has not yet begun work on these issues, since its focus has been on creating the bylaws to govern the work of the Assembly.[82]

No equivalent white paper addresses the MOJ, but some efforts are under way to assess prospects for the reform of key subsectors. The number of active nongovernmental organizations (NGO) and international organizations (IO) efforts focused on justice sector reform suggests that the lack of a roadmap has not limited efforts. Indeed, the Ministry of Justice appears to be less of a black box than the MOI, although civil society groups such as the Tunisian Human Rights League question whether any of these efforts have produced meaningful reform.[83]

One of the first groups to engage with the Ministry of Justice was the Geneva Center for the Democratic Control of the Armed Forces (DCAF). Discussions eventually produced an agreement in October 2011. The scope of the DCAF effort with regard to MOJ reforms includes institutional and legal reform of the penitentiary and re-education system as well as strengthening the capacity of the penitentiary and its personnel.[84] In late January, DCAF met with the Minister of Justice, Noureddine Bhiri, to discuss the implementation of the memorandum of understanding between the ministry and DCAF for prison reform.[85] The UN Development Program (UNDP) and the UN Office of the High Commissioner for Human Rights (OHCHR) are reportedly also engaged in training programs to support prison reform. The United States has also sought to engage on the issue of prison reform, but has not yet signed an agreement with the Tunisian government.

DCAF has also worked with the Ministry of Interior to collect and catalogue laws and amendments relating to the security sector. These texts have been uploaded to an electronic database, accessible in both Arabic and French, which was released to the MOI on January 26, 2012. The index includes legislation relating to the traditional security providers (the military and the police), the justice sector (the courts and prisons), as well as management and oversight of the security sector (government, ministries, parliament, and the courts). Legislation governing the work of political parties, the media, and NGOs was also included.[86] This single, easily accessible, and searchable resource for all laws and amendments pertaining to the security sector greatly enhances the transparency of the legal framework governing the security sector.

Another reform initiative that has garnered international engagement is the training of prosecutors. The UNDP-Tunisia has begun to develop a training program, and the American Bar Association (ABA) Rule of Law Initiative (ROLI) has also sought to offer training for young attorneys that focuses specifically on how to understand their role in a democratic society. Key issues include how to protect the rights of the accused and the political rights of the public.

The challenge of how best to resolve the issue of transitional justice is particularly pressing in Tunisia as public frustration with the apparent lack of progress has grown. While there is a strong impulse for revenge against those who were responsible for the human rights abuses of the Ben Ali regime, there is also widespread recognition that the numbers of individuals who were "tainted" by the Ben Ali regime are so large that the process of bringing them all to justice will likely stretch beyond the current 12-to-18-month transition process. Many acknowledge that amnesty is not politically possible, given the charged nature of the issue today, but people from across the political spectrum also agree that some form of amnesty will be necessary to prevent the construction of a post-Ben Ali Tunisia from being derailed. According to activists at the Tunisian Human Rights League, "Tunisia can't have progress without some reconciliation with the old regime, but the people won't support it."[87]

Ennahda clearly recognizes the importance of judicial accountability for the crimes of the Ben Ali regime and created a new position in Jebali's cabinet. The new Minster for Transitional Justice and Human Rights is Samir Dilou, a lawyer and member of the Executive Bureau of the Ennahda Party. Dilou is also an Ennahda deputy in the Constituent Assembly and the spokesperson for the Jebali government. Implementation of transitional justice is a key issue in the transitional government's agenda. Given the depth of the former regime's corruption and its influence within the judicial system, it remains a question whether justice can be achieved without first implementing extensive internal judicial reform.

A key issue is the corruption of the judicial system. Corruption was rampant, particularly in the last five years of Ben Ali's regime. As one activist noted, "He fell so quickly because not a single family was untouched by the corruption." The corruption extended across the government, not just in the Ministries of Justice and Interior, but also in the Ministries of Agriculture,

Government Property, Commerce, and Industry, to name a few. "At the end," the activist added, "everyone was fed up with the corruption, even in the government. This is why the revolution took only 2 days in Tunis. He [Ben Ali] fled because no one came to his defense."[88] It will be essential to remove the coterie of judges, prosecutors, and lawyers who were loyal to the Ben Ali regime. Practices such as the fixing of sentences before trial will need to be reformed.

Another critical issue for the reform of the justice sector will be assessing whether the body of laws and institutional guidelines sufficiently protect the rights of all citizens and adequately constrain the authority of government entities in accordance with the rule of law. Equally critical will be reforming the institutional and operational culture of the ministry, the judiciary, the prosecutorial services, and the prison system to adhere to these laws and guidelines; training existing personnel how to operate according to these guidelines; and recruiting and training new personnel to fill the mission of the justice sector in accordance with democratic governance and the rule of law.

However, within the Judiciary, and in stark contrast to the Ministry of Interior, there are some indicators that reform has begun. Judges and prosecutors who were known to be corrupt are beginning to be discharged. This is a promising beginning. A draft law removing the President of Tunisia and the Minister of Justice from the Superior Council is also being considered.[89] According to Moussa Abdelsattar, the Director of the Tunisian League of Human Rights, there are five issues that need to be addressed for there to be justice in Tunisia. First, the regime needs to prosecute former regime officials who engaged in human rights violations during the revolution. Second, there needs to be reconciliation between these perpetrators and their victims. Third, the government must establish standards for the adequate compensation of the victims of the former regime. Fourth, it is necessary to implement reform of the security apparatus, the judicial system, and the media. And, finally, there must be assurances that the martyrs of the revolution will be honored appropriately. According to Abdelsattar, progress is being made only on the first element.[90]

Ennahda's leadership has urged patience to allow the judicial system to work and to allow reform of the judicial system to begin to take effect. According to Dilou, it is imperative that the government begin implementing justice while at the same time purging the judiciary of corrupt elements from the former regime.[91] Because the reform process will take time, "it is imperative that we carry on both the reform process and the transitional justice process simultaneously."

Ennahda cannot ignore real demands for justice from the former regime's many victims, who mobilized to overthrow the regime and who expect the new government to hold the perpetrators accountable. Yet, Ennahda does not want to generate the perception that the new government is after revenge. Nor does it want to further undermine the ability of the police to resume legitimate security functions, which will in turn enable the military to return to the barracks. Balancing these issues will require a transparent, inclusive, and incremental process to achieve legitimate justice without making the passive supporters of the Ben Ali regime into a new class of victims and sacrificing Tunisia's present stability.

Civil Society

The final piece of the Tunisian security sector map is civil society, a broad category that includes the media, NGOs, trade unions, and human rights advocacy institutions that promote democratic oversight and transparency of the security sector for ordinary citizens.

Civil society is a bright point in the Tunisian security sector. Since the revolution, the number of civil society groups has exploded. Civil society groups are engaged in issues with relevance across the security sector spectrum, and their efforts, together with public pressure, have been critical in pushing Tunisia's transitional regimes to move forward with reforms. A few examples are worth noting.

While the media have focused on the important part that social networks played in the Tunisian revolution, there are civilian institutions that existed in Tunisia well before the revolution. One of these institutions is the General Tunisian Workers Union (UGTT). Its membership numbers in the hundreds of thousands.[92] The UGTT organized several strikes during the decades of Ben Ali's rule.[93] Institutions like the UGTT that survived the Ben Ali regime with their legitimacy intact will be important actors during the transition period and, unlike many of the new civil society groups, are well organized and well known to Tunisia's citizens.

Tunisians have created new civil society groups to push for transparency and accountability during the transition. Two of these groups are *Le Labo' Democratique* (The Democracy Lab) and OpenGovTN. The Democracy Lab joined with DCAF to organize a conference on the management and disposition of the regime's secret police files. OpenGovTN has focused its activities on the transparency of the National Constituent Assembly and the inclusion of Tunisian citizens during the constitution-drafting process, principally through unrestricted access to Assembly proceedings. Comprised of professional Tunisians and Tunisian expatriates, the organization has developed a series of transparency initiatives—a TV channel that broadcasts the Constituent Assembly meetings live; and publication of the reports of various governmental commissions, the records of the votes of each member of the Constituent Assembly, the record of attendance of Assembly delegates, and the record of the debates and speeches of every member of the Assembly. One goal of OpenGovTN is to provide citizens with information so that they can judge their representatives' competence and hold them accountable in subsequent elections.

An explosion of media outlets is another positive sign of Tunisia's transition to democratic rule. Widely viewed as a mouthpiece of the Ben Ali regime, the media are now adjusting to a freer climate after decades of censorship and repression. The proliferation of cable, radio, and print media is a positive step forward, but media companies claim that the government is dragging its heels during the licensing process. Ennahda has complained that the new Tunisian media establishment has tended toward sensationalist journalism and that it has negatively portrayed the achievements of the government.[94] Some argue that government scrutiny of the media is necessary because the explosion of new media companies threatens journalistic integrity. Media advocacy groups such as the International Freedom of Expression Exchange have organized conferences on the role of the media in a democratic society, access to information, and media independence.[95] Similarly, the Independent National Authority to Reform Information and Communication (INRIC), which seeks "protection of the right of the Tunisian people to a free, pluralistic and transparent media," has submitted 14 recommendations for a press code to the government and has engaged in advocacy to establish new regulations to reorganize the media and to prevent the emergence of monopolies.[96] Ennahda's leadership has recognized the need for the reform of government control of the media, and has reached out to the British Broadcasting Corporation (BBC) as a potential model for Tunisia.[97]

Recommendations for the Way Ahead

Successful democratic transitions require the achievement of four key goals:[98] First, sufficient agreement has to be reached about the political process to produce an elected government. This has been achieved. Second, the elected government must come to power through a free and fair vote. This, too, has been accomplished. Third, the government must have de facto authority to generate new policies. This, too, has been achieved by all three of Tunisia's transition governments. Fourth, the executive, legislative, and judicial authorities of the new government cannot be required *de jure* to share power with other bodies (for example, the military, or in Tunisia, the police).[99] This, too, has been accomplished, although in practice the government faces serious challenges asserting its legal authority over key elements of the Ben Ali regime, notably the Ministry of Interior and, to a lesser extent, the Ministry of Justice.

These accomplishments are remarkable. Tunisia has achieved in 1 year what none of the other Arab Spring states has been able to. This leaves Tunisia well poised to undertake serious security sector reform. Reform will be essential for Tunisia's security sector to transition from a black box whose *raison d'être* was protecting the regime, to transparent and democratically accountable institutions whose primary mission is to protect the people. There are four priority actions to be accomplished:

1. The first priority is to restructure the internal security services and the Ministry of Interior. The labyrinth of internal security institutions and the lack of transparency over the most basic issues—a ministerial organizational chart, official numbers of interior forces—suggest that reform of the internal security sector must begin with a mapping of the institutions, the forces, and the personnel and assessing exactly what is required for effective reform. The white paper is a good start. The caretaker government should draw on the expertise of Tunisian and international experts to ensure that the mapping and assessment of the internal security forces and the Ministry of Interior are robust and that the proposed reforms meet Tunisia's security needs. With greater transparency in place, it will be possible to address the three remaining reforms.

The first is establishing democratic oversight over the Ministry of Interior, to include executive oversight by the minister and parliamentary oversight over the ministry's practices, budgets, and reform plans. Implementing these reforms will require a fundamental reorientation of the ministry's institutional culture and mission. The second needed internal security sector reform is divesting, reorganizing, and retraining the internal security and police forces to create a new police service that conducts humane, accountable, responsive, and capable policing. The third necessary reform is resolving the Ministry of Interior and the police forces' "image problem." The white paper suggests new uniforms, new logos, and more welcoming reception areas in police stations.

These are important tangible indicators of change. They must be accompanied by real change; that is, fundamental reorientation in how the ministry and its forces engage with citizens and with the democratically elected executive authorities and parliament. The restoration of police services will also help restore both the confidence of the police and the public's trust in the government.

2. A second priority is to establish the governance and democratic oversight of the security sector. The creation of bylaws to govern the constitution-drafting process, and recognition that the process needs to be transparent, are positive developments. As the National Constituent Assembly begins drafting a new constitution, critical issues for SSR include creating the legal framework that establishes permanent oversight by both the executive and the parliament over the security sector. A central element of this framework will be the creation of parliamentary committees on defense, security, and intelligence. One of the recently created constitutional commissions has drafting authority for the committees on law enforcement and security. A particular challenge during the coming year is how this oversight, particularly of the reform efforts of the security sector, will be conducted while the new constitution is being written. The one institution with a true electoral mandate during the transitional period is the National Constituent Assembly. Its oversight over the reform process during this transitional year will be important for the legitimacy of the SSR in Tunisia.

3. A third priority is to reform the justice sector, including the Ministry of Justice, the Judiciary, and prosecution services. Because there is no roadmap yet for the reform of the justice sector, developing an assessment is a good place to start. Discussions have already begun over prison reform and prosecutor training. The role of the Judicial Police and the apparent lack of investigative capabilities either in the MOI or the MOJ are clear priorities, and international technical assistance and training might be useful to begin addressing these gaps. As in the MOI, Ministry of Justice reform will likely require reorienting the institutional culture of the ministry and retraining judges, prosecutors, lawyers, court clerks, notaries, bailiffs, and many others. This is an enormous project that could well stretch over a decade.

4. The final priority is to manage the difficult issue of transitional justice. Although transitional justice is not itself part of security sector reform, it is intricately connected to it. Transitional justice involves resolving difficult, and often emotional, issues that resonate throughout Tunisia, including whether to prosecute members of the former Ben Ali regime, and if so, who exactly should be prosecuted; whether to purge the ministries and which ones; and

whether and how to compensate the victims of the former regime. How transitional justice is addressed in Tunisia will have great bearing on how SSR efforts proceed.

Closely related to transitional justice is the way to vet the state administration across all the ministries, but particularly Interior, Justice, and the Judiciary. The MOI's inability to remove senior officials in the ministry suggests that civilian control over the ministry is a pressing issue. The lack of judicial independence, particularly the executive's authority over the appointment, reassignment, and promotion of judges and prosecutors is another challenge. The vetting of the state administration is a delicate issue that involves balancing the need to purge certain key positions or senior levels of individuals tainted by the former regime against the risk of creating a new aggrieved minority—if the purges are too extensive—or of losing the ability to deliver major services. In the case of the Judiciary, the risk is to undermine the legitimacy of the judicial system and the rule of law.

Another related question is whether to prosecute those individuals who are to be purged and others for their activities under the previous regime, or to grant them amnesty. Transitional justice can provide a good foundation for longer-term judicial reform. Support from international experts with experience managing transitional justice elsewhere might be useful, if the Tunisian leadership should request the expertise. Ennahda's leadership is certainly aware of the challenges, and has taken great pains to emphasize that anything that smacks of revenge will be counterproductive. Ennahda seeks reconciliation, not revenge.

That SSR is a highly political process is frequently underappreciated. In any political process, there are winners and losers, and the potential losers of Tunisian SSR were among the most privileged in Tunisian society. What is frequently overestimated is the value of security. The assumption is that once basic security is restored, "the rest will fall into place." This is by no means a necessary given. While Tunisia's relatively smooth transition from revolution to a democratically elected caretaker government is remarkable, much remains to be done. Serious reform of the security sector remains essential if Tunisia's transition to democratic rule is to succeed in the long term.

End Notes

[1] Hernando de Soto, "The Real Mohammad Bouazizi," Foreign Policy, December 16, 2011, available from www.foreign-policy Rania Abouzeid, "Bouazizi: The Man Who Set Himself

and Tunisia on Fire," Time.com, January 21, 2011, available from www.time.com /time/magazine/article /0,9171, 2044723, 00.html. Early media reports mistakenly reported that Mohammad Bouazizi had a university degree.

[2] "Al Arabiya Inquiry Reveals How Tunisia's Ben Ali Escaped to Saudi Arabia," Al Arabiya January 13, 2012, available from www.alarabiya.net/articles/2012/01/31/188093.html.

[3] William MacLean, "Tunisia Army Pivotal to Ben Ali Ousting: Reports," Reuters, January 17, 2011, available from www.reuters.com/article/2011/01/17/us-tunisia-protests-army-idUS-TRE70G52B20110117.

[4] Philippe Droz-Vincent, "A Return of Armies to the Forefront of Arab Politics?" IAI Working Papers 11/21, July 2011, p. 8.

[5] Heiner Hänggi, "Conceptualising Security Sector Reform and Reconstruction," in Allan Bryden and Heiner Hänggi, eds., Reform and Reconstruction of the Security Sector, Münster: Lit, 2004; Sean McFate, "Securing the Future: A Primer on Security Sector Reform in Conflict Countries," United States Institute of Peace Special Report 2009, September 2008.

[6] Alexis Arieff, "Political Transition in Tunisia," CRS Report for Congress RS 21666, December 16, 2011, p. 2.

[7] Tunisian Ministry of Defense, "The Role of the Tunisian Armed Forces During the Revolution," transcript of the ministry briefing, Tunis, January 24, 2012, p. 4. Since February 2011, about 1,600,000 refugees, mostly from sub-Saharan Africa, have fled the fighting in Libya and have streamed across the Tunisia-Libya border crossing-points at Ras Jdir and Dhiba. The Tunisian Army is still playing an active role in managing this situation, knowing that more than 3,000 refugees from sub-Saharan countries are still present in the Choucha camp, while [an]other 325,000 Libyans are living in different regions within Tunisia [sic]. The refugee camps are located in Choucha, Ras Jedir, Tataouine, Remada, and Dhiba.

[8] Author interviews with senior military officers, Tunis, Tunisia, January 23-25, 2012. (Hereafter, Author interview(s), January 23-25, 2012.)

[9] Author Interview with Dr. Radwan Masmoudi, Tunis, Tunisia, January 23, 2012.

[10] Author interview, Tunis, Tunisia, January 23, 2012.

[11] Omar Mestiri, director of Radio Kalima, quoted in Asmar Ghribi, "Tunisia Media Reform: An Incomplete Process," Tunisia-Live.net, December 30, 2011, available from www.tunisia-live. net/2011/12/30/tunisian-media

[12] Ibid.

[13] Mark Sedra, "Security Sector Transformation in North Africa and the Middle East," United States Institute of Peace Special Report 296, November 2011.

[14] Fernanda Faria and Alvaro Vasconcelos, "Security in Northern Africa: Ambiguity and Reality," Chaillot Paper Series no. 25, September 1996, p. 24.

[15] Ibid.

[16] Author interviews, January 23-25, 2012.

[17] International Institute for Strategic Studies, "The Middle East and North Africa," in The Military Balance 2012, Vol. 112, No. 1, London, UK: Routledge, 2012, p. 352; Ellen Knickmeyer, "Just Whose Side Are Arab Armies On, Anyway?" Pulitzer Center on Crisis Reporting, January 28, 2011, available from pulitzercenter. org/articles/arab-armies-tunisia-military

[18] Ministry of Defense Brief, January 24, 2012.

[19] "Middle East and North Africa," in The Military Balance 2011, London, UK: International Institute for Strategic Studies, 2011, pp. 293-342.

[20] Author interviews, January 23-25, 2012.

[21] Briefing and interview by author with a joint panel of senior military officers at the Ministry of Defense, Tunis, Tunisia, January 24, 2012.

[22] Author interviews, January 23-25, 2012.

[23] Author interview with Mohammad Lazhar Akremi, Tunis, Tunisia, January 25, 2012.

[24] Author interview, Tunisia, January 23, 2012.

[25] Charles Baeder, "Release of Unauthenticated Prison-Sex Video Denounced in Defense of Tunisian Interior Minister," Tunisia-Live.net, January 19, 2012, available from www. tunisia-live.net/2012/01/19/release-of-unauthenticated-prison-sex denounced-in-defense-of-tunisian-interior-minister/.

[26] "Al Arabiya Inquiry Reveals How Tunisia's Ben Ali Escaped to Saudi Arabia," Al Arabiya, January 13, 2012, available from www.alarabiya.net/articles/2012/01/31/188093.html.

[27] Author interview with members of the Tunisian Young Lawyer's Association, Tunis, Tunisia, January 24, 2012.

[28] H. Mzioudet, "Former Tunisian Chief of Presidential Security Reveals: 'Gaddafi Provided Ben Ali Police With Tear Gas Bombs'," TunisiaLive.Net, November 3, 2011, available from www.tunisia-live.net/2011/11/03/former-tunisian-chief-of-presidentialsecurity-reveals-gaddafi-provided-ben-ali-police

[29] "Al Arabiya Inquiry Reveals How Tunisia's Ben Ali Escaped to Saudi Arabia."

[30] Sana Ajmi, "In Tunis, Protest Against Security Forces Union Open Strike," Live-Tunisia.net, February 2, 2012, available from www.tunisia-live.net/2012/02/02/in-tunis-protest-against-security-forces-union-open-strike/.

[31] Ibid.

[32] Ibid.

[33] Quoted in William G. O'Neill, "Police Reform in Tunisia: The Revolution Must Continue," draft report, January 31, 2012.

[34] Author interview with senior Ennahda party official, Tunis, Tunisia, January 25, 2012.

[35] Geneva Centre for the Democratic Control of Armed Forces (DCAF), "Assessment of the Communication of the Ministry of Interior," DCAF, October 5, 2011, full report available from www.rapprochement.org, trans. by Google Translate, January 19, 2012.

[36] "Conference on Secret Police Archives," DCAF-, November 16, 2011, available from dcaf-tunisie.org/ en/2011/11/16/conference-on-the-archives-of-the-political-police/.

[37] Republic of Tunisia Ministry of Interior Mohammad Lazhar Akremi, "Security and Development: A White Paper for Democratic Security in Tunisia," November 21, 2011, available from Graeme Carroll and Winnie Tsang, trans. Official copies in Arabic and French.

[38] Author interview with Mohammad Lazhar Akremi, Tunis, Tunisia, January 25, 2012.

[39] Akremi, "Preface," in "Security and Development: A White Paper for Democratic Security in Tunisia,", p. 4.

[40] Ibid., p. 5.

[41] Ibid., p. 6.

[42] Ibid., p. 12.

[43] Ibid., pp. 13-15.

44 Author interview with members of the Ennahda Political Bureau, Tunis, Tunisia, January 25, 2012.

[45] "Security and Development: A White Paper for Democratic Security in Tunisia," p. 27.

[46] Ibid.

[47] Ibid., p. 29.

[48] Author interviews, Tunis, Tunisia, January 24, 2012.

[49] "Security and Development: A White Paper for Democratic Security in Tunisia," p. 28.

[50] Ibid., p. 30.

[51] Author interview with DCAF, Tunis, Tunisia, January 23, 2012.

[52] Aidan Wills, Guidebook: Understanding Intelligence Oversight, Geneva, Switzerland: Center for the Democratic Control of Armed Forces, 2010, p. 9.

[53] Amine Ghali, "Tunisia's Moment of Opportunity," Project on Middle East Democracy, January 28, 2011, p. 2, available from pomed.org/blog/2011/01/new-pomed-policy-

[54] "Timeline: Tunisia Goes to the Polls," Reuters, October 23, 2011, available from www.reuters.com/article/2011/10/23/us-tunisiavote-events-idUSTRE79M0ZI20111023.

[55] Jason Gluck, "Constitutional Reform in Transitional States: Challenges and Opportunities Facing Egypt and Tunisia," USIP Peace Brief 92, April 29, 2011, p. 3.

[56] "Tunisia's Election Winners Form Interim Government after Uprising," The Guardian, November 21, 2011, available from www.guardian ennahda-ettakatol.

[57] Sana Ajmi, "Tunisia's Populist Surprise Headed for Marginalization in Constituent Assembly," TunisiaLive.net, November 10, 2011, available from www.tunisia-live.net/2011/11/10/ the-position-of-al-aridha-in-the-tunisian-constituent-assembly/.

[58] Tarek Amara, "Tunisia's Constitutional Assembly, Elected after a Revolution that Inspired the 'Arab Spring' Uprisings, Held its Opening Session on Tuesday, Described by Officials as an Historic Step Toward Democracy," Reuters, November 22, 2011, available from www.reuters.com/article/2011/11/22/us-tunisiaassembly-idUSTRE7AL2AI20111122.

[59] Asma Ghribi, "Tunisian Prime Minister Declares Interim Government's Intention to Hold Presidential Elections in 18 Months," Tunisia-Live.net, February 3, 2012, available from www.tunisia-live.net/2012/02/03/tunisian-prime-minister-declares- interim-governments-intention-to-hold-presidential-elections-in18-months/.

[60] The possible timing of the elections remains uncertain. In an interview with Tunisian daily La Presse published on March 28, 2012, Jebali recognized that conflicting statements had been made regarding the timing of the national elections. He noted that the government has asked the National Constituent Assembly to establish a timetable for its activities. "We sincerely hope that the Assembly accelerates the process of drafting the constitution. . . . As a government, we believe that the next elections should not exceed June 2013. It is preferable that they be held on April 9 or at the end of June after the completion of the school year. This would allow the new government to begin operations in September 2013 without any disruption." See Samira Dami and Néjib Ouerghi, "Le combat du Tunisien n'est pas de savoir s'il est musulman ou non,"("The struggle of the Tunisian person is not to know whether he is muslim or not.") La Presse, Tunisia, March 28, 2012, available from www.lapresse.tn/28032012/47543/ le-combat-du-tunisien-nest-pas-de-savoir-sil-est-musulman-ou-non. html. For an alternate timeline suggested by Jebali's aide, see Kouichi Shirayangai, "Tunisia Scheduled to Hold Parliamentary Elections on or Before March 20, 2013," Tunisia-Live.net, March 24, 2012, available from www.tunisia-live.net/2012/03/24/tunisia- scheduled-to-hold-parliamentary-elections-on-or-beforemarch-20-2013/.

[61] The Tunisian Government Portal, The Ministry of National Defense, available from www.tunisie.gov.tn/index.php?option=com_ ministeres&Itemid=382&task=view&id=28&lang=english.

[62] Author interview with human rights activists, Tunisia, January 23, 2012.

[63] Author interview, Tunis, Tunisia, January 24, 2012.

[64] Alfred Stepan, "Tunisia's election: counter-revolution or democratic transition?" New York: The Immanent Frame, Social Science Research Council, available from blogs.ssrc.org/ tif/2011/12/17/tunisia%E2%80%99s-election-counter-revolution- or-democratic-transition/.

[65] Ibid.

[66] Amine Ghali, "Tunisia's Moment of Opportunity," pp. 2-3.

[67] Author interview, Tunis, Tunisia, January 25, 2012.

[68] Rules of Procedure of the National Constituent Assembly, adopted January 20, 2012.

[69] Author interview with Duncan Pickard, Washington, DC, February 29, 2012.

[70] Helen Keskes, "Tunisia: Constituent Assembly Members Vote in Favor of Transparency," AllAfrica.com, January 7, 2012, available from allafrica.com/stories/201201070044.html.

[71] Ministry of Justice Portal, "Attributions," available from www.e-justice.tn.

[72] Presidential Decree No. 74-1062. See Ibid.

[73] Ibid.

[74] Ministry of Justice Portal, "General Directorate of Prisons and Rehabilitation," available from www.e-justice.tn.

[75] Author interview, Tunis, Tunisia, January 23, 2012.

[76] Ministry of Justice Portal, "Prisons et Centres de Rééducation," available from www.e-justice.tn.

[77] Nathan Brown, "Arab Judicial Structures: Tunisia," UNDP Programme on Governance in the Arab Region (POGAR), available from www.pogar.org/publications/judiciary /nbrown/tunisia.html.

[78] Article 65, "Independence of Judiciary," Constitution of the Republic of Tunisia, adopted June 1, 1959, and amended July 12, 1988, available from unpan1.un.org/intradoc/groups/public/ documents/cafrad/unpan004842.pdf.

[79] Luca Perilli, "Independent and Impartial Professional Justice," Jean-Marie Beney, David Forest, Michael Groepper, Christian Johnson, James McManus, Luca Perilli, Marie-Francoise Verdun, and Pierre Weiss, Final Report: EU Diagnosis Mission of the Tunisian Judicial and Prison System, Peer Review, Brussels, Belgium: European Commission, December 2011, Chap. 4.

[80] Ibid., "Executive Summary."

[81] Author interview with members of the Youth Lawyers Association and the Lawyers Union, Tunis, Tunisia, January 24, 2012.

[82] Ibid.

[83] Author interview with the Tunisian League of Human Rights, Tunis, Tunisia, January 23, 2012.

[84] "The Tunisian Ministry of Justice and DCAF Sign an Agreement Protocol for Cooperation in the Reform of the Penitentiary System," Geneva Centre for the Democratic Control of Armed Forces, DCAF-Tunisie, October 5, 2011, available from dcaf-tunisie.org /en /2011/10/07/the-ministry-of-justice-and-dcaf-sign-a-memorandum-of-understanding-for-cooperation-in-prison-system-reform/?utm_source=rss&utm_medium=rss&utm_campaign =the-ministry-of-justice-and-dcaf-sign-a-memorandumof-understanding-for-cooperation-in-prison-system-reform.

[85] The Minister of Justice Speaks with DCAF about Prison Reform," DCAF, January 26, 2011, available from www.DCAF-tunisie.org.

[86] Author interviews with DCAF representatives in Tunis, Tunisia, January 23-25, 2012. Database is available from www. legislation.

[87] Author interview Tunisian Human Rights League, Tunis, Tunisia, January 23, 2012.

[88] Author interviews with civil society activists and political party leaders, Tunis, Tunisia, January 23, 2012.

[89] Author interviews, Tunis and Washington, DC, February 2012.

[90] Hanen Keskes, "Transitional Justice Process in Post-Revolutionary Tunisia," Tunisia-Live.net, January 30, 2012, available from www.tunisia-live.net/2012/01/30/transitional-justice-process-inpost-revolutionary-tunisia/.

[91] Ibid.

[92] Christopher Alexander, "Opportunities, Organizations, and Ideas: Islamists and Workers in Tunisia and Algeria," International Journal of Middle East Studies, Vol. 32, No. 4, November 2000, pp. 465-490.

[93] Eric Lee and Benjamin Weinthal, "Trade Unions: The Revolutionary Social Network at Play in Egypt and Tunisia," Guardian.co.uk, February 10, 2012, available from www.guardian.co.uk/ commentisfree/2011/feb/10/trade-unions-egypt-tunisia/print.

[94] Author interview with Ennahda party members, January 25, 2012.

[95] Asma Ghribi, "Tunisian Media Reform: An Incomplete Process," Tunisia Live-net, December 30, 2011, available from www.tunisia-live.net/2011/12/30/tunisian-media incomplete-process/.

[96] "INRIC-Protect the Right of the Tunisians to a Free, Pluralistic and Fair Media," September 1, 2011, available from www. nawaat.org.

[97] Author interview with members of the Ennahda Political Bureau, Tunis, Tunisia, January 25, 2012.

[98] Stepan.

[99] Juan Linz and Alfred Stepan, Problems with Democratic Transitions and Consolidation: Southern Europe, South America, and Post-Communist Europe, Baltimore, MD: Johns Hopkins University Press, 1996. See also Ibid.

INDEX

#

9/11, 27

A

access, 51, 59
accountability, 11, 56, 58
activism, 15
advancement, 46
advocacy, 15, 58, 59
Afghanistan, 13
Africa, 18, 28, 39, 63
agriculture, 19
Air Force, 39, 50
Al Qaeda, 12, 13, 27
Algeria, 10, 12, 20, 27, 67
American Bar Association (ABA), 56
anger, 7, 44
anti-government protests, vii, 1, 5
apex, 54
appointments, 37
Appropriations Act, viii, 2
Appropriations Committee, 14, 28
Arab countries, 17
armed forces, 13, 37, 38, 39, 40, 41, 43, 50
armed groups, 37
arrest(s), 11, 26, 43, 44
assessment, 40, 46, 60, 61
assets, 13, 18, 21, 28
authority(s), 11, 17, 18, 19, 20, 22, 25, 50, 51, 53, 54, 57, 60, 61, 62
Ayman al Zawahiri, 12, 13

B

Bahrain, 31
ban, 35, 52
barriers, 19
base, 6
Belgium, 12, 13, 66
benefits, 12, 17
bilateral aid, viii, 2, 22, 23
blasphemy, 28
blogs, 66
bond market, 23
border crossing, 63
border security, 13, 24
bureaucracy, 31, 35

C

Cabinet, 50
cabinet members, 44
CAF, 64, 66
candidates, 10, 36, 52
cash, viii, 2, 23
catalyst, 32, 35
censorship, 7, 35, 59

challenges, vii, 1, 3, 5, 8, 32, 35, 36, 38, 40, 41, 46, 60, 62
chaos, 5
chemicals, 17
Chicago, 29
Chief of Staff, 35, 50
China, 6
CIA, 6, 26
cities, 34
citizens, 13, 22, 32, 35, 45, 49, 57, 59, 61
citizenship, 7
civil liberties, 14
civil rights, 7
civil society, 4, 23, 31, 35, 36, 37, 38, 45, 49, 51, 52, 55, 58, 67
civil war, 10, 40
clients, 55
climate, 44, 59
clothing, 6
coastal region, vii, 1, 3
codes, 46
codes of conduct, 46
Cold War, 16, 21
colleges, 39
commercial, 26, 54
communication, 22, 45, 46
community(s), 9, 36, 38, 47
compensation, 11, 39, 45, 57
complexity, 25, 42
conference, 9, 23, 58, 64
confession(s), 43
confinement, 10, 14, 54
conflict, 12, 32, 36
confrontation, 16
Congress, viii, 2, 4, 14, 21, 22, 23, 24, 29, 49, 63
consensus, 26
consent, 54
Consolidated Appropriations Act, viii, 2, 23
Constitution, 25, 26, 54, 66
construction, 56
controversial, 5, 14
conversations, 39
conviction, 28
cooperation, 19, 20, 23, 24, 28, 66
corruption, 11, 18, 20, 36, 52, 56
cost, 23
Côte d'Ivoire, 20
counsel, 43, 54
counterterrorism, viii, 2, 14, 20, 22, 43
Counterterrorism Fellowship Program, 33, 39
Coup, 26
credit rating, 17
crimes, 56
criminals, 44
criticism, 22
crowds, 7, 35, 51
Cuba, 14
culture, ix, 6, 32, 34, 38, 46, 50, 57, 60, 61
curriculum, 33

D

database, 55
deaths, 43
decision makers, 47
delegates, 59
democracy, viii, 2, 5, 10, 19, 21, 23, 37
Democratic Party, 4, 15
demonstrations, 5, 7, 9, 10, 16, 22, 34, 40, 43, 52
denial, 14
depth, 56
detention, 7, 14, 54
developed countries, 7
dignity, 21, 22
diplomatic balance, vii, viii, 2
disaster, 12
disorder, 12
disposition, 58
dissatisfaction, 12, 48
dissidents, 7
DNA, 43
DNA testing, 43
Doha, 22
dominance, 5

donors, viii, 2, 20
draft, viii, 1, 2, 10, 45, 48, 49, 52, 53, 57, 64
drug trafficking, 42
due process, 10, 14

E

economic development, 21, 36
economic growth, 6, 17, 25, 29
economic integration, 19, 21
economic policy, 16, 17, 22
economic recovery, viii, 2, 5
economic reform(s), 23
education, 25, 26, 34, 55
Egypt, viii, 2, 12, 23, 31, 35, 40, 65, 67
election, 8, 16, 20, 23, 36, 37, 49, 52, 66
emergency, 17
emergency relief, 17
employment, 17
engineering, 14
environmental conditions, 36
equality, 25
equipment, 6, 24, 40, 44
ethics, 46
EU, 19, 28, 66
euphoria, vii, 1
Europe, 7, 19, 44, 67
European Commission, 28, 66
European Union, 17, 19, 54
evidence, 14, 43
evolution, 25
execution, 53
executive branch, 22
executive function(s), 47
executive power, 53
exercise, 14, 41, 47, 54
exile, 7, 10, 15, 19
expenditures, 40
expertise, 46, 60, 62
exports, 17, 21

F

Facebook, 42
faith, 17, 26
families, 11
family members, 11, 18, 20, 28
FDI, 17
fear(s), 5, 12, 17, 44, 48
financial, viii, 2, 17, 18, 20, 24, 53
financial institutions, viii, 2, 24
financial regulation, 53
financial support, 17, 20, 24
fiscal deficit, 17
food, 16
force, 9, 16, 19, 21, 35, 39, 42, 43, 44
foreign aid, 25
foreign assistance, viii, 2, 22, 24
foreign direct investment, 17, 18
foreign investment, 17
foreign policy, vii, viii, 2, 21, 25
formula, 36
France, 6, 13, 14, 15, 19, 45, 49
free trade, 19, 21
free trade area, 19
freedom, 5, 6, 9, 28, 37
funding, viii, 2, 22, 23, 24, 29
funds, 3, 23

G

gangs, 36
Gaza Strip, 19
GDP, 40
Generalized System of Preferences, 21
Germany, 6, 13
global security, 27
governance, 36, 38, 40, 41, 47, 49, 50, 57, 61
governments, 18, 22, 45, 48, 60, 65
governor, 7, 17
graduate program, 33
grassroots, 10
gross domestic product, 26, 40
growth, 17, 19

Guantanamo, 13, 21
guardian, 65, 67
guidance, 52
guidelines, 57

H

Hamas, 19
harassment, 23
health, 50
heart attack, 52
history, viii, 2, 6, 36, 51
homes, 43
House, 14, 27, 29
housing, 54
human, 6, 14, 15, 19, 20, 28, 32, 36, 44, 46, 50, 53, 55, 56, 57, 58, 65
human right(s), 6, 14, 15, 19, 20, 28, 44, 50, 53, 55, 56, 57, 58, 65
human security, 32, 36
hydrocarbons, 6

I

identity, 8, 9, 10
ideology, 9
image, 46, 60
IMF, 17, 28
immigration, 19
imports, 21
impoverished interior, vii, 1, 3
imprisonment, 46
income, 6, 17
independence, 6, 16, 49, 54, 59, 62, 66
individual rights, 4, 25
individuals, 12, 18, 25, 35, 42, 56, 62
industry, 4, 17
inequality, 4, 17
inflation, 16, 17
infrastructure, 40, 44
inheritance, 7
insects, 26
insecurity, 5, 25, 32, 36
institutions, ix, 4, 8, 32, 34, 35, 36, 38, 39, 41, 47, 58, 60
integrity, 50, 59
intelligence, 11, 22, 37, 38, 45, 46, 47, 61
interest groups, 25
interference, 7, 23, 28
International Monetary Fund, 17
International Narcotics Control, 24
international trade, 18
interrogations, 43, 54
intervention, 26
investment, viii, 2, 17, 19, 21
investors, 4
Iraq, 13
Islam, 5, 8, 9, 10, 12, 26, 27, 37
Islamic law, 8
Islamic state, 13
Islamism, vii, viii, 2
Israel, 19, 28
issues, 4, 5, 15, 21, 24, 25, 46, 53, 55, 56, 57, 58, 60, 61
Italy, 6, 13, 40

J

jihadist, 9
job creation, 25, 29
journalism, 59
journalists, 7, 35
judiciary, 4, 14, 53, 54, 55, 57, 66

L

law enforcement, 53, 61
laws, 7, 8, 36, 47, 55, 57
lawyers, 7, 35, 36, 43, 55, 57, 61
lead, 6, 11, 15, 17, 45
leadership, 15, 16, 44, 57, 59, 62
learning, 37
legality, 14
legislation, viii, 2, 37, 53, 55, 66
liberalization, 6
loan guarantees, 23

loans, 19
loyalty, 51

M

machinery, 6
majority, 6, 26
man, 12, 34, 43, 45, 51
management, 46, 55, 58
manipulation, 18
manpower, 40
manufactured goods, 19
mapping, 42, 60
mass, 10, 14
materials, 38
matter, 41, 50
Mauritania, 13, 20
media, 2, 4, 23, 38, 53, 55, 57, 58, 59, 63, 67
medical, 14, 15
medicine, 15
Mediterranean, 22
membership, 58
middle class, viii, 2, 6, 36
Middle East, 21, 22, 23, 24, 26, 27, 28, 32, 37, 63, 65, 67
military, viii, ix, 2, 7, 10, 13, 20, 21, 24, 27, 31, 34, 35, 36, 37, 39, 40, 41, 44, 47, 50, 55, 58, 60, 63, 64
military aid, 21
military courts, 10
military school, 50
military spending, 40
minorities, 9, 25
mission(s), 39, 40, 41, 47, 57, 60
moderates, 8
modernization, 46
momentum, vii, 1
monetary policy, 17
monopoly, 47
Morocco, 20, 26, 31
MTI, 10
Multilateral, 24
Muslim states, 18
Muslims, 6, 12, 27

N

national security, 25, 40
National Strategy, 33
NATO, 20, 22
neglect, 18
new media, 59
news coverage, 4
NGOs, 55, 58
North Africa, 17, 23, 24, 28, 32, 33, 37, 63

O

Obama, viii, 2, 21, 22, 23, 24
Obama Administration, viii, 2, 23, 24
obstacles, 55
officials, 3, 5, 10, 11, 12, 17, 18, 19, 20, 21, 22, 28, 34, 40, 42, 44, 51, 57, 62
oil, 17
opacity, 46
openness, vii, viii, 2
operations, 12, 20, 43, 65
opportunities, 7
opposition movement, 5
opposition parties, 15, 36, 49
optimization, 46
organize, 25, 58
OSC, 27
Overseas Private Investment Corporation, 24
oversight, ix, 24, 34, 35, 37, 38, 41, 42, 47, 49, 50, 53, 55, 58, 60, 61
ownership, 17

P

Pakistan, 13
Palestinian Authority, 19
parallel, 42
parole, 53
payroll, 42
peace, 39, 40, 41
peacekeeping, 39, 40, 41

perpetrators, 14, 57, 58
platform, 15
playing, 63
pluralism, 10, 53
police, ix, 5, 7, 9, 11, 13, 24, 34, 35, 37, 38, 41, 42, 43, 44, 45, 46, 48, 51, 54, 55, 58, 60, 64
policy, viii, 1, 3, 4, 11, 12, 21, 25, 39, 46, 49, 53, 62, 65
policymakers, viii, 2
political instability, 5, 12
political leaders, 18
political participation, 6
political parties, 2, 19, 23, 31, 35, 37, 51, 55
political party, 9, 14, 15, 26, 67
political system, vii, viii, 2, 6, 8, 9, 25, 40
political uncertainty, 17
politics, 10, 13, 37, 41, 53
polling, 25
popular support, 8
popular vote, 8
population, ix, 6, 7, 9, 13, 32, 34, 35, 36, 38
poverty, 17
presidency, 6, 16, 20
President, vii, 1, 2, 4, 5, 6, 7, 8, 10, 14, 15, 16, 19, 20, 21, 22, 26, 28, 29, 31, 34, 37, 39, 43, 45, 47, 49, 50, 52, 54, 57
President Obama, 21, 22
prevention, 36
principles, 5, 17, 32, 53, 54
prisoners, 2, 48, 54
prisons, 53, 55
private investment, 23
private sector, viii, 2
privileged coastal region, vii, 1, 3
probe, 28
professionalism, 13, 46
programming, 37
project, 33, 61
proliferation, 59
prosperity, 7
protection, 4, 43, 44, 50, 59
PTT, 16
public service, 53
public support, 18

R

radio, 38, 59
RCD, 6, 26, 48, 52
reception, 46, 60
recognition, 19, 49, 56, 61
recommendations, 45, 46, 59
reconciliation, 11, 20, 46, 56, 57, 62
reconstruction, 20
recovery, viii, 2, 5
recruiting, 57
recurrence, 32, 36
redistribution, 46
reform(s), v, vii, ix, 1, 3, 5, 11, 14, 17, 26, 29, 31, 32, 33, 34, 36, 37, 38, 40, 41, 45, 46, 47, 48, 50, 51, 52, 54, 55, 56, 57, 58, 59, 60, 61, 62, 63, 64, 65, 66, 67
refugee camps, 37, 63
refugees, 37, 40, 63
regional policy, 21
regulations, 59
rehabilitation, 53, 54
relatives, 3, 7
relevance, 58
relief, 19, 23
religion, 4, 5, 8, 9, 10, 53
repression, 7, 10, 16, 20, 59
repressive security services, vii, viii, 2
reserves, 17
resource management, 46
resources, 13, 51
response, 5, 22, 29, 35, 40
restoration, 61
restrictions, 2, 6, 15
retribution, 43
rights, 7, 10, 15, 16, 35, 53, 56, 57
risk, 5, 22, 62
root(s), 5, 12, 13
rule of law, 15, 32, 36, 38, 53, 57, 62

rules, ix, 34, 53
rural areas, 43

S

safety, 38
Saudi Arabia, 5, 7, 35, 63, 64
school, 15, 37, 65
science, 52
scope, 41, 50, 55
security, vii, viii, ix, 1, 2, 3, 5, 6, 10, 11, 12, 13, 19, 20, 23, 24, 25, 27, 32, 33, 34, 35, 36, 37, 38, 39, 40, 41, 42, 43, 44, 45, 46, 47, 48, 50, 51, 52, 53, 55, 57, 58, 60, 61, 62, 64
security assistance, 23
security forces, 10, 13, 19, 35, 39, 40, 42, 43, 45, 50, 60
Security sector reform (SSR), ix, 34, 36
security services, vii, viii, ix, 2, 4, 6, 11, 12, 13, 25, 27, 34, 35, 40, 46, 60
security threats, 4
seizure, 26
Senate, 28
services, 11, 19, 38, 46, 50, 53, 57, 61, 62
sex, 64
shape, vii, viii, 2, 4, 5, 25, 49
Sharia, 9, 12, 54
Shiites, 26
signs, 11
smuggling, 12, 26
social contract, 32, 35, 38
social network, 58
society, vii, viii, 2, 16, 36, 37, 43, 56, 58, 59, 62
socioeconomic status, 7
South Africa, 46, 49
South America, 67
sowing, 11
SP, 21
Spain, 6, 13, 45
speech, 5, 21, 22, 36
spending, 26
Spring, ix, 24, 28, 31, 32, 34, 38, 60, 65
stability, 19, 27, 35, 40, 58
stabilization, viii, 2
staffing, 11
state, viii, 2, 4, 7, 8, 9, 11, 13, 16, 17, 18, 19, 20, 29, 31, 32, 35, 36, 37, 38, 39, 41, 46, 47, 60, 62
state of emergency, 7, 35
State of the Union address, 22
statehood, 19
statistics, 42
strategic planning, 50
structure, 4, 11
sub-Saharan Africa, 37, 40, 63
suicide, 14
Sunnis, 26
suppression, 43
surplus, 20
surveillance, 7, 11, 22, 46
Switzerland, 45, 65
Syria, viii, 2, 12, 18, 21, 31

T

tangible benefits, 5
tanks, 41
TAP, 28
target, 17
technical assistance, 61
techniques, 46
television stations, 37
tension(s), vii, 1, 3, 4, 10, 11, 20
tenure, 33
territory, viii, 2, 6, 36, 50
terrorism, 13, 14
terrorist activities, 12
terrorist organization, 9
terrorists, 13
textiles, 6
threats, 9, 25
time constraints, 55
time frame, 52
torture, 11, 27, 43, 44
tourism, 4, 17
trade, viii, 2, 5, 10, 19, 21, 23, 58, 67
trade benefits, 19

trade preference, 21
trade union, 5, 10, 58
trafficking, 12
training, ix, 15, 24, 25, 34, 36, 42, 44, 46, 50, 54, 55, 56, 57, 61
training programs, 55
trajectory, 25
transformation, 38, 46
transition period, 58
transparency, ix, 34, 38, 40, 46, 47, 52, 53, 56, 58, 60
trial, 14, 43, 57
Tunisian Armed Forces, ix, 34, 39, 40, 41, 49, 63
Turkey, 18

U

U.S. policy, 21, 24
UK, 63
UN, 40, 52, 55
UNDP, 55, 56, 66
unions, 4, 16, 51, 67
United, viii, 2, 12, 13, 20, 22, 24, 25, 32, 39, 40, 55, 63
United Nations, 40
United States, viii, 2, 12, 13, 20, 22, 24, 25, 32, 39, 55, 63
urban, 6, 7, 12, 43
urban areas, 7, 43

V

vacuum, 5, 37
vehicles, 44
victims, 11, 57, 58, 62
violence, 5, 9, 12, 13, 35, 37, 43
violent extremist, 26
vote, viii, 1, 10, 25, 60
voters, 25

W

wages, 16
war, 39, 50
Washington, 21, 27, 29, 33, 66, 67
water, 39, 43
weakness, 44
weapons, 12, 40, 42
wear, 37
West Africa, 24
West Bank, 19
Western Europe, 13
White House, 21, 28, 29
White Paper, 45, 64, 65
workers, 25
working conditions, 44
World Bank, 6, 28, 29
World Trade Organization, 28
World War I, 21

Y

Yemen, 31
youth unemployment, 35

